Critical Guides to French Texts

64 Sartre: La Nausée

Critical Guides to French Texts

EDITED BY ROGER LITTLE, WOLFGANG VAN EMDEN, DAVID WILLIAMS

SARTRE

La Nausée

Paul Reed

Lecturer in French
University of Keele

Grant & Cutler Ltd
1987

© Grant & Cutler Ltd
1987

Library of Congress Cataloging-in-Publication Data

Reed, Paul, 1940-
  Sartre, La nausée.

  (Critical guides to French texts: 64)
  Bibliography: p.
  1. Sartre, Jean Paul, 1905-1980. Nausée. I. Title. II. Title: Nausée.
  III. Series.
PQ2637.A82N3374 1987 843'.914 87-23708
ISBN 0-7293-0272-5 (pbk.)

I.S.B.N. 84-599-2170-0

DEPÓSITO LEGAL: V. 2.583 - 1987

Printed in Spain by
Artes Gráficas Soler, S.A., Valencia
for
GRANT & CUTLER LTD
55-57, GREAT MARLBOROUGH STREET, LONDON W1V 2AY
and
27, SOUTH MAIN STREET, WOLFEBORO, NH 03894-2069, USA

Contents

Preface   7

Introduction   9

1. Existence and Nausea   15
        The world   16
        People   23

2. Essences and the Bourgeoisie   31
        Behaviour and the social order   33
        Identity and the social image   36
        Ethics and the social norm   38

3. Existence and Art   41
        L'Etre-en-soi   41
        L'Etre-pour-soi   46
        Art   49

4. The Art of *La Nausée*   57
        Characterisation   60
        Form   63
        Language   67

Conclusion: *La Nausée* and the Literary Tradition   74

Select Bibliography   79

To Theresa

Preface

The fact that philosophy is an integral part of *La Nausée* makes it an intellectually demanding novel. In an attempt to illuminate the subtleties of the text, I have referred fairly extensively to Sartre's philosophical works, with the result that the present critical guide is more a guide than a critique. Although less attention has been given to the novel as literature than it unquestionably deserves, my hope is that the somewhat non-literary approach adopted will nevertheless lead to an enhanced appreciation and a just evaluation of Sartre's literary achievement.

References to the text of *La Nausée* are to the Folio edition. References of the type: (*12*, p.24) are to items listed in the bibliography.

This study has benefited considerably from my discussions of *La Nausée* with a colleague, Dr Roger McLure. I should like to thank him for so readily placing at my disposal his time and philosophical expertise. My thanks are also due to another colleague, Dr Ruth Murphy, for her constructive comments on the presentation of my arguments.

P.R.

Introduction

There were three Sartres: the compulsive writer, the professional philosopher and the committed socialist. The first two worked well together. The arrival of the third partner, however, gave rise to certain tensions. Although these were productively harnessed to begin with, they proved in the longer term, and by Sartre's own very exacting standards, to be irreconcilable.

The first of the trio to appear on the scene was the writer. Sartre reveals in *Les Mots*, his autobiography of his childhood, that his early years were dominated by the imaginary world of schoolboy adventure-stories. These served as a substitute for the real world, from which he was isolated as a child, and quickly became a literary model for his own artistic endeavours. When a friend of his mother's solemnly predicted of the seven-year-old prodigy: 'Ce petit écrira!' (*12*, p.127), there seemed to be no going back. Sartre the writer was born. The philosopher came into existence in 1923, when the eighteen-year-old Sartre, who was then preparing the entrance examination for the Ecole Normale Supérieure, read Bergson's *Essai sur les données immédiates de la conscience*: 'C'est devenu une vocation à partir de Bergson, c'est-à-dire que j'ai senti le besoin de faire ça, tout en ne sachant pas très bien quel rapport il y avait entre philosophie et littérature' (*14*, p.41). In 1931, Sartre became a teacher of philosophy and remained in the profession until 1944, when he resigned from his post at the Lycée Condorcet in Paris to devote himself full time to writing.

Sartre's career as a teacher had already been interrupted, between 1939 and 1941, by war service. The experience was to have a profound influence on his future development both as a writer and as a philosopher. In an interview he gave to mark the occasion of his seventieth birthday, he described the war years as a decisive turning-point in his life: 'C'est là, si vous voulez, que je suis passé de l'individualisme et de l'individu pur d'avant la guerre au social, au socialisme' (*15*, p.180). Military call-up had impressed upon Sartre the inescapable fact of his involvement in society. Suddenly, he had discovered that his life had a social dimension: the artist was also a man who lived in the real world. Soon after the war, Sartre published *Qu'est-ce que la littérature?* (*10*), in which he argued that the task of the prose writer was to bear witness to the fundamental problems of his own time; prose literature should thus become an instrument for social change and not be simply an object of aesthetic contemplation. The trio was now complete.

La Nausée was composed before the war by the writer and philosopher and was Sartre's first serious attempt at literature. He started work on it soon after taking up an appointment at the *lycée* of Le Havre in 1931. The town, which boasted both an hôtel Printania and a municipal library complete with its resident *autodidacte*, provided the basic model for Bouville. Except for the 1933-34 session, spent at the Institut Français in Berlin, Sartre remained at Le Havre until 1936. He worked on *La Nausée* throughout that period.

The various stages of the novel's composition have been recorded by Simone de Beauvoir in her memoirs. She and Sartre had met as students in 1929 and were to become life-long partners. It was to Beauvoir, already known to her student friends as 'le Castor', that Sartre dedicated his novel. His ambition in writing *La Nausée* was, in Beauvoir's words, to express 'sous une forme littéraire des vérités et des sentiments métaphysiques' (*17*, p.293). Sartre's own account, while confirming Beauvoir's, places slightly greater emphasis on the philosophical dimension: 'ça représente... la mise en forme d'une idée philosophique... Si je ne l'avais pas rendue sous cette forme romanesque, l'idée n'était pas encore assez solide pour que j'en fasse un livre philosophique' (*3*, pp.1699-1700). His main objective, then, was to use literary expression to give, both for himself and the reader, palpable reality to certain metaphysical intuitions. These intuitions were to form the basis of the philosophical system which was to follow with the publication of *L'Etre et le néant* in 1943.

The difficulties of combining literature and philosophy were pinpointed by Beauvoir's comments on the first version of the novel: 'C'était une longue et abstraite méditation sur la contingence. J'insistai pour que Sartre donnât à la découverte de Roquantin [*sic*] une dimension romanesque, pour qu'il introduisît dans son récit un peu du *suspense* qui nous plaisait dans les romans policiers' (*17*, p.111). And so the poetic revelation of contingency still lacked elements proper to the novel form. The incorporation of these was the subject of a revision of the novel during Sartre's year in Berlin. Beauvoir was favourably impressed with the result but still felt that 'Sartre avait abusé des adjectifs et des comparaisons' (*17*, p.209). On his return to Le Havre, Sartre set to work on yet another version, which he finished early in 1936 and submitted to the publishers, Gallimard.

The novel was turned down. The following year, however, it was read by Gaston Gallimard personally, whose only reservations concerned the title. Sartre had called the novel 'Melancholia' after the engraving by the German artist, Dürer. This title would have stressed the theme of the inadequacy of human knowledge to explain existence, since the engraving depicts a brooding figure, surrounded by a welter of objects, among which instruments, some of them scientific, figure prominently. The alternative title proposed by Sartre, 'Les Aventures extraordinaires d'Antoine Roquentin', fortunately left Gallimard equally unimpressed. The definitive title was Gallimard's own idea, and *La Nausée* was finally published in April 1938.

Sartre had thought highly of his novel and had been bitterly disappointed by its initial rejection. In a conversation with John Gerassi in 1973, he described how he had felt at the time: 'ça m'a fait quelque chose: je m'étais mis tout entier dans ce livre et j'y avais travaillé longtemps; en le refusant c'était moi-même qu'on refusait, c'était mon expérience qu'on excluait' (*3*, p.li). Soon after the war, however, Sartre was to voice certain reservations about his earlier achievement. In the 1950s, he became aware of the true extent to which his views, particularly about literature, had been conditioned by his bourgeois upbringing and education. The former had shielded him from the harsher realities of life, such as material deprivation; the latter, from the influence of Marx and Freud. In an interview he gave to *Le Monde* following the publication of *Les Mots* in 1964, Sartre compared himself to the writer he had been in the thirties: 'Ce qui me manquait c'était le sens de la réalité. J'ai changé depuis. J'ai fait un lent apprentissage du réel. J'ai vu des enfants mourir de faim. En face d'un enfant qui meurt, *La Nausée* ne fait pas le poids' (*13*, p.13). This last statement was not intended as a repudiation of either the artistic merit or the philosophical content of *La Nausée*; for in 1972 Sartre still maintained that '*La Nausée*... c'est le goût de l'existence pour l'homme... même dans une société entièrement désaliénée' (*3*, p.1669). Sartre's point was rather an ideological one: literature had more urgent tasks than to reveal the 'taste' of contingent existence, which, in a hungry world, was a delicacy that could be ill-afforded.

In *Les Mots* itself, Sartre's comments on *La Nausée* bear on his attitude to writing at that time, the autobiography being concerned with the motives which had lain behind his decision to dedicate his life to literature. His discovery was that he had grown up believing literature to be the highest form of human activity and that he himself had been born to write. Consequently, while revealing to his fellow men the unjustifiability of their existence, he saw his own existence as justified by the creation of the work of art:

> Je réussis à trente ans ce beau coup: d'écrire dans *La Nausée* — bien sincèrement, on peut me croire — l'existence injustifiée, saumâtre de mes congénères et mettre la mienne hors de cause. *J'étais* Roquentin, je montrais en lui, sans complaisance, la trame de ma vie; en même temps j'étais *moi*, l'élu, annaliste des enfers, photo-microscope de verre et d'acier penché sur mes propres sirops protoplasmiques. (*12*, pp.209-10)

In short, Sartre felt in retrospect that he had indirectly adopted the aesthetic solution tentatively considered by Roquentin at the end of *La Nausée*: the man was redeemable by the disembodied artist.

What may seem puzzling is Sartre's failure to recognise, until the 1950s, that he himself had opted for a solution contemplated by one of his own characters some twenty years previously. The explanation of the mystery lies in the difference between Sartre's novel and Roquentin's projected novel. In his seventieth-birthday interview Sartre described thus his attitude at the time of writing *La Nausée*: 'Dire la vérité sur l'existence et démystifier les mensonges bourgeois c'était tout un et c'était ça que j'avais à faire pour accomplir mon destin d'homme, puisque j'avais été fait pour écrire' (*15*, p.177). Consequently, Sartre's mission as a writer had a philosophical dimension with far-reaching moral implications, a dimension which Roquentin's projected novel, being a purely artistic venture, lacks. Immediately after the war, Sartre's theory of committed literature had presumably allowed him to go on seeing his literary activity as a social obligation rather than as the 'neurosis' later diagnosed in *Les Mots*. In the fifties, however, when, in his own words, Sartre was 'thrown into the atmosphere of action', writing began to appear as an unprivileged form of activity and this, coupled with doubts about its political efficacy, caused Sartre to question his own literary activity and subsequently to abandon literature altogether.

When Sartre discussed *La Nausée* in his seventieth-birthday interview, it was again in terms of its political relevance. In the 1964 interview, Sartre had argued from an ideological stand-point that the philosophical dimension of *La Nausée* was untimely: existential problems could wait until the advent of a socialist society. In the later interview, in 1975, he saw the philo-sophical dimension not merely as historically premature but as philosophically incomplete. *La Nausée* had attacked the bourgeois as a self-deceiving individual, whereas Sartre later came to appreciate that 'on ne peut comprendre un individu, quel qu'il soit, qu'en le voyant comme un être social. Tout homme est politique' (*15*, p.176). Roquentin himself had been presented purely as an individual, for whom authenticity involved a complete withdrawal from society rather than being something achieved through solidarity with his fellow human-beings. Roquentin/Sartre was 'l'individu qui s'oppose à la société par l'indépendance de sa pensée mais qui ne doit rien à la société et sur qui celle-ci ne peut rien, parce qu'il est libre' (*15*, p.176). The moral implications of *La Nausée* were, then, largely negative: a repudiation of bad faith rather than an affirmation of authenticity.

After the war, the writer and the philosopher were drawn into the orbit of the socialist. The philosopher evolved and provided a theoretical basis for the arguments of the socialist. The artist, also, adapted to the new circumstances but was later called to account, found wanting and dismissed. One might have expected *La Nausée* to suffer a similar consignment to oblivion. But, on the contrary, it continued to occupy a special place in Sartre's affections. True, the philosophical dimension was later felt to be too restricted, but it was resorbed, and not rejected, by the later philosopher. Moreover, it is arguable that the aesthetic unity of *La Nausée* is dependent upon the 'narrow', purely metaphysical approach to philosophy. Long after he had said his 'farewell to literature' with *Les Mots*, Sartre was to acknowledge in a conversation with Michel Contat and Michael Rybalka, the editors of the Pléiade edition of his novels, his predilection for his first novel: 'Dans le fond, je reste fidèle à une chose, c'est à *La Nausée*... C'est ce que j'ai fait de meilleur' (*3*, p.1669).

1. Existence and Nausea

Roquentin's diary entry for the day following his decision to abandon his biography of Rollebon is brief and to the point: 'Rien. Existé' (p.147). It is not that Roquentin has ever doubted either his own existence or that of the external world, but never before has he so strongly experienced his own bodily existence and the sheer materiality of the world of objects. The next day, during his lunch with the Autodidacte, he explicitly identifies this intuition of pure existence with his attacks of nausea: 'C'est donc ça la Nausée: cette aveuglante évidence? Me suis-je creusé la tête! En ai-je écrit! Maintenant je sais: J'existe — le monde existe — et je sais que le monde existe' (p.173).

The culminating revelation of the world of things will not occur until later, when Roquentin gazes at the tree root in the park. On writing up that experience he explains why he has taken so long to discover the seemingly obvious: 'à l'ordinaire l'existence se cache' (p.179). Sartre will make the same point, and in almost the same words, five years later in his major philosophical work, *L'Etre et le néant*: 'l'être des existants est ordinairement voilé' (*6*, p.464). In that work Sartre argues that the materiality of existence is masked owing to the way in which consciousness functions under normal conditions. *La Nausée*, however, is a study of an abnormal state. By the time Roquentin starts to keep a diary, his relationship to the world and to other people has already begun to change, and the normal relationship is alluded to only occasionally, as a measure of this change. It is to *L'Etre et le néant*, therefore, that we must turn for a fuller description of the normal functioning of consciousness.

Although the changes which occur in Roquentin's perception of objects, of the self and of other people are discussed separately in the present chapter, it must be stressed that, in Sartre's philosophical system, the world and man form an indivisible whole. Their inseparability is evident in his description of human reality as *l'être-dans-le-monde*. Sartre rejects the traditional subject-object dualism, in which the mind and the world are conceived as independent entities. So-called objective reality, he argues, is never purely objective: the reality of an object is the way it appears to a subject. Neither can there be a pure subject: Sartrean consciousness is a 'nothingness', an immaterial being which needs the world in order to exist at all. For Sartre, 'l'homme et le monde *sont* des êtres relatifs et le principe de leur être *est* la relation... Surgir, pour moi, c'est déplier mes distances aux choses et par là même faire qu'il y ait des choses' (*6*, p.370). In other words, we do not first of all discover that we have a mind which we then direct at the world to uncover its meaning. Consciousness and the world emerge simultaneously.

The world

Any comparison between *La Nausée* and *L'Etre et le néant* is complicated by Sartre's tendency in the latter to use words in a specialised way. We may note, for example, the change from 'l'existence' to 'l'être des existants' in the two quotations compared earlier. The word *monde*, too, acquires a special meaning in Sartre's philosophy. When he affirms that it is only through the presence of an individual consciousness that 'there are things', he is clearly not adopting the position of the idealist, for whom material reality is a creation of the mind. Rather, he is making a distinction, central to the presentation of material reality in *La Nausée*, between the fact that matter is, independently of the human presence, and the fact that it is a spatially located consciousness which causes individual objects to stand out as such. Without perspective, objects would sink into an 'indistinction totale' (*6*, p.371). Thus, the phrase 'qu'il y ait des choses' has a special value in the above context. Thinking in terms of the English equivalent of *il y a*, we may put the matter thus: things *are*, independently of an observer; but since *there* presupposes a relation to *here*, I can only say that *there are* things, because I am *here*. To distinguish between material existence as it is in itself and material existence as it appears to an individual consciousness, Sartre will use the terms *être-en-soi* and *monde* respectively.

How then does the world appear to consciousness? It is argued in *L'Etre et le néant* that consciousness invariably projects itself on to the world as a series of tasks to be undertaken. It therefore sees the world in terms of the means of performing these tasks; that is to say, it organises the world on a practical basis around itself as a centre of reference: 'l'espace originel qui se découvre à moi... est sillonné de chemins et de routes, il est instrumental et il est le *site* des outils' (*6*, p.386). Just as the world is a practical arrangement of existence from my point of view, so individual objects acquire significance for me in terms of their usefulness or their resistance to my projects or possible projects. Consequently, objects do not appear to us merely as things but are spontaneously perceived in terms of their function: 'la chose n'est point d'abord chose pour être ensuite ustensile, elle n'est point d'abord ustensile pour se dévoiler ensuite comme chose: elle est *chose-ustensile*' (*6*, p.250).

Meaning is not, therefore, inherent in existence but is a function of the objectives that an individual consciousness sets itself. Sartre argues, for instance, that an ink-bottle is such only because I *use* it and is breakable only in the light of the possibility of my throwing it at something hard. In itself, it is undifferentiated from the mass of being and is neither a determinate object (a bottle), nor has it a function (a container for ink), nor has it potentiality (it can be broken). In itself, it simply is (*6*, p.246). But because a consciousness spontaneously constitutes being into a world of tasks waiting to be performed, we attribute to being what properly belongs to consciousness:

> Dans ce que nous appellerons le monde de l'immédiat, qui se livre à notre conscience irréfléchie, nous ne nous apparaissons pas *d'abord* pour être jetés *ensuite* dans des entreprises. Mais notre être est immédiatement 'en situation', c'est-à-dire qu'il *surgit* dans des entreprises et se connaît d'abord en tant qu'il se reflète sur ces entreprises.

> Nous nous découvrons donc dans un monde peuplé
> d'exigences. (*6*, p.76)

We necessarily project ourselves on the world in this way, because consciousness, being a 'nothingness', can define itself only in terms of the world; and yet, such self-projection is not registered on the immediate level of awareness (*la conscience irréfléchie*) because, as we shall see in Chapter Three and as our own experience regularly testifies, we are primarily aware of what lies outside us and not of ourselves.

It is this spontaneous ordering of material being on an instrumental basis which masks existence. But we order being in other ways, too, through the formulation of scientific laws and through language. Existence will be revealed in its true, brute state, only if these ordering processes break down, if consciousness itself begins to falter. This is precisely what happens in Roquentin's case.

His first recorded attack of nausea occurs while he is out walking on the beach. He picks up a pebble to throw into the sea but, suddenly and inexplicably overcome with revulsion, he drops it. He is afterwards unable to recall why, but a series of further attacks gradually uncovers the truth. The process of revelation reaches its climax in the park, and when Roquentin later attempts to put his experience into words, he thinks back to the way things used to appear to him: 'Même quand je regardais les choses, j'étais à cent lieues de songer qu'elles existaient: elles m'apparaissaient comme un décor. Je les prenais dans mes mains, elles me servaient d'outils, je prévoyais leurs résistances. Mais tout ça se passait à la surface' (p.179). It is now the sheer existence of things which impresses itself on Roquentin: objects are no longer perceived as *choses-ustensiles* but simply as *choses*. He is at last able to explain why he dropped the pebble: 'j'ai senti qu'il *existait*... de temps en temps les objets se mettent à vous exister dans la main' (p.173).

It may seem paradoxical that a pebble should trigger off his nausea, when later attacks are induced by organic forms of existence, by people in restaurants or by plants in parks, and minerals themselves are the least disquieting of existing things. However, it is the very solidity of the pebble which first alerts

Roquentin to the basic materiality of objects. As a natural object, the pebble lacks the obvious instrumentality of an artefact. Moreover, Roquentin does not even hold the pebble as something he intends throwing into the sea, but with 'les doigts très écartés' (p.12). It is primarily a cold, hard 'thing' which is in contact with his fingers. After his encounter with the pebble, other objects begin to force themselves on Roquentin's attention: 'Les objets, cela ne devrait pas *toucher*, puisque cela ne vit pas. On s'en sert, on les remet en place, on vit au milieu d'eux: ils sont utiles, rien de plus. Et moi, ils me touchent, c'est insupportable. J'ai peur d'entrer en contact avec eux tout comme s'ils étaient des bêtes vivantes' (p.24). Objects are no longer confined to their normal, passive roles as instruments but have acquired an independent existence. Roquentin finds the resulting contiguity so threatening and repulsive that he can no longer indulge in his favourite pastime of picking up anything that happens to be lying on the ground (pp.22-23).

Roquentin's visit to the café Mably one foggy Friday morning contributes to his growing alienation from objects. Quite naturally, the fog causes things to lose their clear outlines and become ill-defined. As a result, they now appear to Roquentin 'affaiblies', 'instables' (p.112). Earlier, it was the sense of touch which had predominated in his awareness of objects: he had felt the pebble in his hand as something essentially physical. Here, the impact of objects is visual. Sight, of course, is the least physical of the senses; this time it is the very identity of objects and our efforts to conceptualise them which are undermined. Consequently, Roquentin's growing obsession with the materiality of objects is accompanied by a gradual loss of intellectual control over them. The episode thus constitutes a significant stage in the destructuring of existence experienced by Roquentin.

It is not just the fog which unnerves him. The failure of Fasquelle, the café owner, to put in his usual, early-morning appearance is equally disorientating. Fasquelle had always been Roquentin's guarantee that life conforms to a pattern: 'dans les cafés, tout est toujours normal et particulièrement au café Mably, à cause du gérant, M. Fasquelle, qui porte sur sa figure

un air de canaillerie bien positif et rassurant' (p.18). In other
words, Fasquelle and his café reflect at the social level the
cosmic order in which the bourgeois so blindly believes.
Roquentin seeks a refuge from this hiccup in the social order by
fleeing to the public library, which represents the safe order of
science. But not even this immersion in the accumulated wisdom
of the ages can counter the combined effects on Roquentin's
beleaguered imagination of a February fog and a Fasquelle gone
missing, presumed dead!

He now fears that nature herself may defy the laws of science:
'C'est par paresse, je suppose, que le monde se ressemble d'un
jour à l'autre. Aujourd'hui, il avait l'air de vouloir changer. Et
alors *tout*, *tout* pouvait arriver' (pp.112-13). By the time
Roquentin is due to leave Bouville for good, such speculation
about nature has grown into a conviction: 'Je sais que sa sou-
mission est paresse, je sais qu'elle n'a pas de lois... Elle n'a que
des habitudes et elle peut en changer demain' (p.221). The world
does change, though only, of course, in Roquentin's
imagination: he becomes a prey to surrealistic visions of clothes
that come alive and tongues that turn into centipedes.

Roquentin appears to be implying that because scientific laws
are based on past observations and, consequently, may be
invalidated by what happens in the future, then the so-called
laws of nature do not really exist. However, this is not quite the
conclusion that Sartre wishes us to draw; an indication, perhaps,
that he has not avoided, in this instance, the dangers of combining philosophy and literature. Sartre himself would not have
argued that absolutely anything can happen. The dominant
characteristic of natural objects in the park description was listlessness. The inference to be drawn from the description, and it
will be discussed more fully in Chapter Three, is that material
being is inert; it cannot change itself but can only be acted upon.
Elsewhere, in *L'Existentialisme est un humanisme* for instance,
Sartre stresses that only human beings have the power to change
themselves and are, in this respect, radically different from
cauliflowers (*8*, p.23) — from conkers, too, despite the good job
Roquentin makes of disguising the fact. The latter's assertions
are not, therefore, to be taken too literally.

How, then, should we take them? Firstly, as literature. The changes imagined by Roquentin constitute a dramatic climax to the novel's psychological dimension. His nightmarish visions are the ultimate expression of an almost pathological sense of insecurity vis-à-vis material objects, an insecurity which has a philosophical foundation, even if the visions themselves do not. In short, the lack of rational justification for the laws of science is not being philosophically demonstrated by Sartre but is being exploited for a literary purpose.

At the same time, however, a serious philosophical point is being made; but it concerns the bourgeoisie's misuse of science rather than science itself. The bourgeois sees the laws of nature as pre-established, as prior to nature's existence. These laws are adduced as proof of a cosmic design. Sartre's view, however, is that the laws of nature are not independent of matter in the way that the laws of society, for example, are distinct from the individuals who obey or break them. Scientific laws do not *determine* the behaviour of matter, they *are* the behaviour of matter. Sartre will make the point in *L'Etre et le néant* that an electric current 'n'a pas d'envers secret: il n'est rien que l'ensemble des actions physico-chimiques... qui le manifestent' (6, p.11). Similarly, the laws of nature are exhausted by their manifestation.

Roquentin's assimilation of nature's behaviour to human behaviour, through such words as 'paresse' and 'habitudes', points to a confusion in bourgeois thinking concerning the different kinds of laws. The confusion has already been established, in an ironic vein, by Roquentin himself, through a deliberate mixing of social practice and natural process: the closure of the park at six o'clock in summer is made to appear as inevitable as the melting of lead at 335° (p.221). What complicates matters, and makes the text over-subtle, is that, in the extracts under discussion, a very real similarity between the natural and human worlds underlies the non-valid one imagined by the bourgeois: neither world is subject to pre-established laws, laws which have always been there, even before nature and man themselves. It is for this reason that Roquentin can say that nature has no laws, the laws in question being *a priori* laws. The bourgeois, then, confuses social 'laws', which regulate human behaviour, with scientific laws, which describe the behaviour of natural objects, and both with *a priori* laws. The difference between the first two kinds of law is, of course, considerable. The difference between the first two and the last is even more so, for, as Roquentin has discovered in the park, *a priori* laws do not apply to anything that exists. But more will be said about this in Chapter Three.

Language, too, like science, may cause us to make false assumptions about existence. It does not so much reveal existence as determine the kind of world we see. Words set up a barrier between ourselves and material reality. Roquentin concludes from his experience in the park that thinking about existence distances us from it: 'Quand je croyais y penser, il faut croire que je ne pensais rien, j'avais la tête vide, ou tout juste un mot dans la tête, le mot "être" ' (p.179). Language is, in fact, an abstracting activity. This is most obvious in the way a common noun reduces a unique object to a type. Thus, when we look at a seat, we do not normally see it in its concrete individuality but as an example of a kind; we tend to see only what it has in common with certain other objects of its kind, with other seats. Again, in our use of adjectives, we tend to classify things into reassuring family groups. For instance, whenever Roquentin used to think of the sea, it was in terms of 'appartenance' (p.179): it belonged to the category of green objects. But this was already to perform an abstracting operation which distanced him from existence. Green things as such do not really exist, since no object is purely and simply green and nothing else. In other words, greenness is an abstraction. Because language masks the existence of objects, a symptom of Roquentin's nausea, as an intuition of existence, will be the failure of words to signify.

After his first attack of nausea, Roquentin tries to reconstitute the experience by describing the carton which contains his ink-bottle. But the words, particularly since they reduce the object to a pure form, immediately dispel the sense of the unfamiliar which had accompanied the pebble incident: 'c'est un parallélipipède rectangle... il n'y a rien à en dire... il ne faut pas mettre de l'étrange où il n'y a rien' (p.11). Later in the novel, after

Roquentin has left the library in a panic, he resorts to naming objects in order to counter the threat of transformation: 'Tant que je pourrais fixer les objets, il ne se produirait rien... je me disais avec force: c'est un bec de gaz, c'est une borne-fontaine' (p.114). But as the nausea tightens its hold, words provide an increasingly inadequate defence against existence. Eventually, objects free themselves from language completely, as Roquentin watches the tram-seat lose its identity to resemble the belly of a dead donkey: 'Je murmure: c'est une banquette, un peu comme un exorcisme. Mais le mot reste sur mes lèvres: il refuse d'aller se poser sur la chose' (p.176). Immediately afterwards, the park episode brings matters to a head.

Normally, then, we see existence through the grids of instrumentality, of science and of language. The last two are themselves regarded by Sartre as instrumental, as essentially means of controlling reality rather than of revealing or explaining it. Roquentin's consciousness fails to implement these ordering processes; in Sartrean terms, it fails to transcend existence as materiality. Why the revelation of existence as shapeless, redundant matter should give rise to nausea will be discussed later in the chapter. For the moment, we shall concern ourselves with the fact that it is people rather than objects, and above all himself, who make Roquentin feel most sick.

People

I pointed out earlier in the chapter that on the immediate level of awareness (*la conscience irréfléchie*) we are primarily conscious of what is outside us rather than of a self. When we run after a bus, for example, we are conscious of the bus having to be caught and not of ourselves running. And since 'la conscience de l'homme *en action* est conscience irréfléchie' (*6*, p.74), Roquentin's nausea, the result of acute self-awareness, usually occurs during periods of idleness. These are suitably frequent, for Roquentin enjoys the enviable luxury of working only when he feels like it.

Two of the occasions on which Roquentin becomes acutely aware of his own existence are overtly compared by him. One, described near the beginning of the novel, is his recollection of the experience involving Mercier in Indo-China (which later in the novel becomes Shanghai). The other is the Monday on which he abandons his biography of Rollebon. All of a sudden, Roquentin stops seeing Mercier's invitation purely as an opportunity not to be missed and begins to relate it to the need to make a personal decision. In other words, he becomes aware of himself as an individual in a particular place at a particular time without good reason: 'Je ne parvenais pas à comprendre pourquoi j'étais en Indochine' (p.17). The same process of self-discovery recurs during the second incident. So long as Roquentin was engaged in the biography project, he was not conscious of himself as existing. He vividly portrays his every gesture as having gone towards sustaining the existence of a 'Dracula' Rollebon: 'Je n'étais qu'un moyen de le faire vivre, il était ma raison d'être, il m'avait délivré de moi' (p.140). But now that Rollebon has died for the second time, Roquentin senses a new presence in the room: 'il reste *quelque chose* dans la chambre tiède, quelque chose que je ne veux pas voir' (p.140). This 'something' is Roquentin himself.

What makes his self-awareness so unbearably acute is the fact that, as well as being conscious of himself as an 'I' (as a *conscience réfléchie*), he physically feels, and even tastes, his bodily existence. In the earlier of the two incidents, he had felt as if his body were filled with luke-warm milk (p.17). The later one involves a similar sensation, though this time the milk has been diluted into something less identifiable: 'la chose, qui attendait, s'est alertée, elle a fondu sur moi, elle se coule en moi, j'en suis plein' (p.141). This reduction of his own existence to bodily sensations was already a factor in Roquentin's localised attack of nausea on the beach. He afterwards recalls that the pebble had given him 'une sorte de nausée dans les mains' (p.24). Normally, when we touch things, we are more aware of what we touch than of our hand: 'ma main me révèle la résistance des objets, leur dureté ou leur mollesse et non *elle-même*' (6, p.366). As Sartre's analysis of desire in *L'Etre et le néant* stresses, it is when we are touched by other people, and not when we touch, that we are most aware of our own bodies. But even when we actively touch an object, it is, in a sense, also touching us, since it is in contact with our hand. It is this physical contact which makes Roquentin hypersensitive to the existence of his hands and which subsequently gives him the impression that objects actively touch him (p.24).

Having abandoned his book and discovered his own existence, Roquentin becomes fascinated by his own saliva, which he is obliged perpetually to swallow. His choice of verbs to describe the sensation underlines the close affinity between the sense of touch and the sense of taste: 'Il y a de l'eau mousseuse dans ma bouche. Je l'avale, elle glisse dans ma gorge, elle me caresse... une petite mare d'eau blanchâtre — discrète — qui frôle ma langue' (p.141). It is precisely the taste of oneself in the act of swallowing which Sartre singles out in *L'Etre et le néant* as the archetypal experience of nausea (*6*, p.404). Paradoxically, this singularly undramatic act marks the culmination of Roquentin's self-awareness. There are, of course, much more dramatic things to come before the diary entry ends, but even the commonplace experience of swallowing stands out as exceptional. It does so largely owing to Sartre's skilful manipulation of Roquentin's awareness of time.

Roquentin has by now come to realise that material existence is confined to the present: 'La vraie nature du présent se dévoilait: il était ce qui existe, et tout ce qui n'était pas présent n'existait pas' (p.137). Since his nausea is brought on by the materiality of existence, his attacks will be most virulent if his temporal awareness is restricted to the present. Consequently, Sartre gradually severs Roquentin's links with both the past and the future. On three separate occasions, Roquentin is made to feel 'délaissé dans le présent'. He uses the phrase twice: when he unsuccessfully tries to revive his past, prior to the Autodidacte's visit (p.54), and when he takes the decision to abandon the biography (p.136). On the latter occasion, he applies the phrase to a similar experience *Chez Camille*, when he had also felt that his past was irrevocably lost (p.97). This imprisonment within the present is identified with a confinement to his bodily existence: he is 'limité à [son] corps' (p.54).

Roquentin feels that his past is disintegrating because his

memories have, like ours, grown dimmer with time. What were once vivid memory-images have now faded into words, which lack the richness and particularity of concrete experience. Sartre himself held that our images of the past are not things which are stored away in the mind to be subsequently consulted in an act of remembering. This accounts for Roquentin's inability to reproduce his memories. He can only reconstruct them, an operation which yields unsatisfactory results for him: 'Je construis mes souvenirs avec mon présent... Le passé, j'essaie en vain de le rejoindre: je ne peux pas m'échapper' (p.54). No longer able to revive a dead past, he is thrown back on a purely physical present: 'Jamais je n'ai eu si fort qu'aujourd'hui le sentiment d'être sans dimensions secrètes, limité à mon corps, aux pensées légères qui montent de lui comme des bulles' (p.54). When Roquentin abandons the biography, the disappearance of the past is made more dramatic by a change in perspective. This time, he focuses not on the deficiency of memory-images but on the total absence of the past from material existence. Looking at the words he has just written, he feels estranged from them. The dried ink does not even contain any trace of its earlier wetness. It is only for his consciousness that the dry ink is ink which has *become* dry. Another example of the physical non-existence of the past is provided by Sartre's account of destruction in *L'Etre et le néant*. The pile of rubble which is left after a bombardment has razed a city to the ground bears no trace of the city as such. If we could limit our awareness to a pure present, or persuade ourselves that we had never seen buildings and cities, the rubble could in no way appear to us as a destroyed city. Like the wet ink, the destroyed city belongs solely to the realm of consciousness, which is able to transcend what exists and relate it to what does not exist.

It is the failure to preserve his past which leads Roquentin to call into question the value of his work as a historian and then to abandon it. By making this decision, he is severing his links with the future too, because all conscious activity involves a transcendence of the present towards the future. It is the very essence of consciousness to be ahead of itself, as it were, to be what it is not. A specific illustration of this future-orientation, and one which is particularly pertinent to Roquentin's own circumstances, is afforded by *L'Etre et le néant*: 'Prendre un porteplume... c'est... [le] dépasser comme simple existant vers sa potentialité et celle-ci, derechef, vers certains existants futurs qui sont les "mots-devant-être-tracés" et, finalement, le "livre-devant-être-écrit"' (*6*, p.464). Roquentin's biography is a correlate of his future self. Once he denies himself this possibility, time collapses for him into a pure present.

When Roquentin looks at his face in the mirror or at his hands, he is adopting on his own body the viewpoint of another person. Sartre draws a sharp distinction in *L'Etre et le néant* between what we are for ourselves (our *être-pour-soi*) and what we are for others (our *être-pour-autrui*). This distinction applies just as much to the parts of the body as to our person as a whole. Our own experience of our eyes as *seeing* is radically different from our eyes as *seen*, by an optician, for example. What is for us the sense of sight becomes, for the other, a sensory organ. This difference of perspective is strikingly conveyed when Roquentin looks at his eye in the mirror and describes it as 'aveugle' (p.32). Because he is standing so close to the mirror, the eye is not even recognisably human. His entire face loses its human quality and becomes 'une chair fade qui s'épanouit et palpite avec abandon' (p.32). We have seen that Roquentin's nausea is caused by the degradation of his existence to bodily existence. Whenever he is nauseated by other people, or by his own body as it might appear to other people, it is because the body itself has been degraded to pure flesh.

Other people are relatively unimportant in *La Nausée*, at least as people. Roquentin frequently refers to his existence as friendless and solitary. The one meaningful relationship in his life has come to an end, only to be succeeded by a casual, mechanical affair with the proprietress of the *Rendez-vous des Cheminots*. In the course of his working day, he meets only the Autodidacte, a character so lacking in individuality that he will only once be referred to by name — in an 'editorial' footnote. In general, people are observed by Roquentin from a distance and with detachment, frequently in the impersonal setting of cafés and restaurants or during collective rituals like the Sunday walk. As a result, they lose their human dimension and appear as object-like. Now an essential feature of human relations for Sartre is that we do, in fact, reduce the other to an object by our look. However, as Sartre explains in *L'Etre et le néant*, such objectivisation does not make him thinglike in the narrower sense of the word: 'ma perception du corps d'autrui est radicalement différente de ma perception des choses' (*6*, p.412). Although, then, our look suppresses the other's subjectivity, we nevertheless see him as a complete person involved in a meaningful situation; as a 'totalité synthétique', to use Sartre's terminology. Thus, we do not see an arm shoot out, but a person reaching for his drink. The other's body is neither a physical thing nor the outward sign of a mind, but the latter's incarnation.

In *La Nausée*, however, the norm once more becomes the exception: other people tend to be experienced by Roquentin neither as pure subjectivity nor as 'totalité synthétique' but as flesh. Only rarely is the other perceived as a subject, one notable example being the description of Jean Parrottin's portrait: 'Son regard était extraordinaire... ses yeux éblouissants dévoraient toute sa face' (p.127). But such instances of disincarnation serve only to give dramatic effect to a redescription of the other, seen no longer as a 'regard', as pure subjectivity, but as flesh. When Roquentin imagines Parrottin with his eyes closed, the latter loses his intimidating air of authority and becomes a 'chair... vaguement obscène' (p.129). Another device used by Sartre to highlight the materiality of the body is to focus attention on its parts. If we catch sight of an arm or a leg when the rest of the body is hidden, the limb is likely to lose its human character, because we may not transcend its materiality towards the meaning of the activity in which its owner is engaged. The hands of the woman customer at the café Mably, for example, 'couraient le long de sa blouse et sur son cou comme de grosses araignées' (p.105). The spidery fingers will appear again in *L'Etre et le néant*, where their effect is described as 'une désagrégation du corps' (*6*, p.413).

The body, then, frequently appears as flesh in *La Nausée*. The restaurant setting, which is fully exploited by Sartre, allows body behaviour, such as eating and digesting, sometimes with a little love-play thrown in for good measure, to eclipse more conscious activity. Moreover, characters are often presented in a semi-conscious or unconscious state, so that attention is diverted from the eyes to the less expressive, fleshier parts of the face, such as the cheeks. Finally, the body is rarely perceived by Roquentin as a signifying whole but as a collection of disparate parts.

This chapter began by identifying Roquentin's nausea with his apprehension of existence as pure materiality. To exist is, in Roquentin's words, *'être là*, simplement' (p.184). Consciousness being *essentially* embodied, our most immediate experience of 'thereness' is our awareness of our own bodies from the inside as 'un goût fade et sans distance' (*6*, p.404). The body as object, whether our own or someone else's, is most strongly experienced as 'simply being there' when it is apprehended as pure flesh. As for inanimate objects, they appear as pure materiality if they cease to be structured by consciousness and sink back into undifferentiated being. It is the 'thereness' of material reality which reveals its contingency or gratuitousness. Sartre's own definition of 'contingent' is that which is 'sans raison, sans cause et sans nécessité' (*6*, p.713). But more will be said of this in Chapter Three. For the moment, we are only concerned with the fact that it is the contingency of existence which causes nausea. As Roquentin says of his experience in the park: 'Tout est gratuit, ce jardin, cette ville et moi-même. Quand il arrive qu'on s'en rende compte, ça vous tourne le cœur et tout se met à flotter... voilà la Nausée' (p.185).

But why *does* contingency provoke nausea? In *L'Etre et le néant*, Sartre appeals to common experience as evidence of the link between them. Nausea is induced by such things as rotten meat, blood and excrement (*6*, p.404). Now, these are extreme forms of contingent matter: the sight of a severed arm is likely to turn our stomachs because it is more obviously 'just there' as a gratuitous lump of matter than an arm which reaches out for a drink. In Roquentin's case, however, not even the securely attached, if disquietingly limp, arm of the Autodidacte is perceived as an arm but as something strange and repugnant. And so it is with most other things he sets eyes on. Consequently,

insights into the contingency of existence, exceptional and
fleeting in everyday life, if indeed they occur at all, become the
very fabric of Roquentin's experience in *La Nausée*.

In the introduction to her English translation of *L'Etre et le
néant*, Hazel Barnes, referring to *La Nausée*, suggests that 'the
only full exposition of its meaning would be the total volume of
Being and Nothingness' (7, p.xvii). Although there is much truth
in this view, it disguises the fact that *L'Etre et le néant* is in many
ways a mirror image of *La Nausée*. While the former is devoted
largely to an account of how, in normal experience, consciousness actively constructs a world, the latter shows what happens
to the world when consciousness begins to run down. The task
facing Sartre the novelist was to find a way of rendering
Roquentin's transition from normality to abnormality that was
both plausible and relevant to the reader's own experience. This
problem will be discussed in Chapter Four.

2. Essences and the Bourgeoisie

The diary proper is preceded by a *Feuillet sans date* which is divided into two parts. The first part contains an account of the experience on the beach, which inspires the diary project. The second part provides confirmation of Roquentin's return to normality and, at the same time, constitutes a description of the bourgeois mentality, for Roquentin refers to himself as feeling 'bien à l'aise, bien bourgeoisement dans le monde' (p.13). This apparent self-identification with the bourgeois is, however, short-lived, being confined to the *Feuillet sans date* itself. The epigraph to the novel has already presented Roquentin as an outsider, as an individual who cannot be identified with a particular social group; who is, in Céline's words, 'sans importance collective'. His use of the word 'bourgeoisement' in no way, therefore, implies a sense of solidarity with the middle classes, but indicates rather an attempt to convey more fully, and not without irony, his regained peace of mind.

It could even be argued that the word has a largely aesthetic significance, for the function of the *Feuillet sans date* as a whole is to highlight the opposition between the experience of nausea, which gives rise to anxiety, and the bourgeois's sense of security, which is induced by the familiar world of human routine. In this way, Sartre establishes at the outset the basic incompatibility between nausea and the bourgeois outlook. The progress of Roquentin's nausea will indeed be accompanied by a growing alienation from the bourgeois world. As for the initial affinity between Roquentin and the bourgeoisie, it provides a structurally satisfying point of departure for the polarisation of the two viewpoints and at the same time allows Roquentin to describe the lure of the bourgeois mentality at first hand.

The incompatibility of viewpoint is not confined to the social sphere but indicates a more fundamental, philosophical opposition, between the existentialist viewpoint and what Sartre calls 'the spirit of seriousness'. Roquentin's anxiety is that of exist-entialist man in general, for whom existence is beyond explan-ation, a fact which gives rise to disorientation and anguish. The 'serious man', on the other hand, believes that meaning is written into nature or prescribed by God, and he derives comfort from this belief. Sartre defines the serious man's attitude in the closing pages of *L'Etre et le néant*: 'l'esprit de sérieux a pour double caractéristique, en effet, de considérer les valeurs comme des données transcendantes, indépendantes de la subjectivité humaine, et de transférer le caractère "désirable", de la structure ontologique des choses à leur simple constitution matérielle' (*6*, p.721).

The two aspects of the spirit of seriousness are equally rele-vant to *La Nausée*, but most of Sartre's commentators confine their remarks to the first of these aspects, owing to its more obvious bearing on the question of morality. For the same reason, Sartre himself does so when he discusses the spirit of seriousness in *L'Existentialisme est un humanisme*: 'il est nécessaire... pour qu'il y ait une morale, une société, un monde policé, que certaines valeurs soient prises au sérieux et considérées comme existant *a priori*; il faut qu'il soit obligatoire *a priori* d'être honnête, de ne pas mentir, de ne pas battre sa femme, de faire des enfants' (*8*, p.34). Clearly, Sartre rejects this view: values are not pre-established, they are not already there waiting to be discovered by a consciousness as soon as it emerges in the world. For Sartre, man is the creator of values; in other words, consciousness, not God or nature, is their source. The second aspect of the spirit of seriousness is a corollary of the first, in that it posits objects as intrinsically desirable, and so value is again dissociated from human subjectivity. To assign desirability to the material composition of objects is to place desirability on a par with an object's physical properties. The latter may feature in descriptions, such as those of the scientist, which make no reference to human subjectivity, whereas desirability itself is an affective quality taken on by objects when they are evaluated in the light of human ends, as instrumental to the achievement of these ends. Bread, for example, is seen by the 'serious' person as something intrinsically good. Its value, however, is relative to the human objective of staying alive. For someone who is anxious to end his life it will have no value whatsoever. In short, the 'serious attitude' gives rise to a confusion of value with fact; it mistakes for pre-given creations of God or nature what is created by human consciousness.

Sartre's account of desirability respects the total freedom of the individual consciousness to decide what is desirable or of value. Bourgeois ideology, on the other hand, places value in the object and subordinates the subjective to the objective. It is this order of priorities which lies at the heart of Sartre's antipathy to the middle-class mentality. The refusal to recognise that human reality is, in its very essence, freedom is reflected in the conventional and authoritarian nature of bourgeois society. In *La Nausée* itself, conformism and authoritarianism are the main targets of social criticism. The first is manifested in the way the bourgeois behaves and in the kind of identity he projects; the second is most obvious in the beliefs he holds and inculcates in others.

Behaviour and the social order

What convinces the Roquentin of the *Feuillet sans date* that he is safe from any further attacks of nausea is the predictability of daily or weekly routine. The familiar sounds outside his window and the clockwork regularity of the public-transport system have a therapeutic effect on him. The reduction of life to familiar patterns eliminates all sense of strangeness and creates the comforting illusion of a carefully regulated cosmos. Roquentin is able to dismiss his earlier anxiety as groundless: 'Qu'ai-je à craindre d'un monde si régulier?' (p.13) and can confidently look forward to the arrival of the last tram of the evening.

The same sense of order is apparent in the time-honoured rituals of Sunday. Indeed, the opening description of the Sunday entry (pp.64-65) has much in common with the second half of the *Feuillet sans date*: tram journeys figure prominently, Roquentin feels able to describe scenes he is not directly witnessing and there is a shift to the future tense. These features point to a total lack of spontaneity in the lives of the townspeople. Conformity of behaviour is the key-note of both the morning and afternoon descriptions. During the morning the hordes converge on the town as if in response to a summons: 'dans toutes les maisons... dans tous les faubourgs' (p.64). Similarly, Sunday afternoon is 'celle que cent mille Bouvillois allaient vivre en commun' (p.77). But not only do all the people do the same thing, they do it all the time. It is during the lunch-time period that the invariability of the Sunday routine is emphasised, when there is a shift away from the Sunday crowds to the individual restaurant *habitués*. Sunday is sauerkraut day for the old men (p.72), and the married couple must have 'their' table (pp.72-73).

The universality of Sunday, coupled with its invariability, endows an arbitrary social routine with the illusion of necessity. The social order is confused with the order of creation. Roquentin himself is guilty of such confusion in the *Feuillet sans date*, when he treats the arrival of the gentleman from Rouen as evidence of 'un monde régulier' (p.13). For the Bouvillois, certain activities are prescribed for Sunday, the range of options being laid down in advance: 'Le dimanche on va au cimetière monumental, ou bien l'on rend visite à des parents, ou bien, si l'on est tout à fait libre, on va se promener sur la Jetée' (p.78). In a historically Christian country like France, Sunday is by tradition different from the rest of the week. And yet what strikes the reader most about Roquentin's account of Sunday is that its religious significance is completely overshadowed by its social dimension. For the bourgeois himself, however, the two are as one. The validity of the social order is guaranteed by God. If the world was created, it must conform to the intentions of an all-powerful creator. And if the Bouvillois enjoy material prosperity, it is owing to 'la protection du ciel' (p.67). Material success is not so much an obstacle to divine election as a proof of it.

The belief in a divinely ordered world where rights and duties exist objectively and where each individual has his allotted role is the theme of the entry devoted to Roquentin's visit to the Portrait Gallery, the second of the two major descriptions of the bourgeoisie in the novel. Here the accent is on self-justification,

the conviction of each member of the élite that he has the right
to exist, that his personal existence was called forth and justified
by his role within the social order, the necessity of which is
grounded in divine creation. This sense of a personal destiny is
not, however, confined to the élite. During his lunch with the
Autodidacte, Roquentin has already been struck by the 'airs
sérieux' of the other customers, who are similarly convinced of
their own necessity: 'il n'en est pas un qui ne se croie indispensable à quelqu'un ou à quelque chose' (p.158). But this sense
of mission is particularly strong in society's leaders, since their
usefulness allows them to regard their existence as indispensable
to the proper functioning of society and, on the private level, to
the management of the family business. In *Situations III*, Sartre
offers the following description of their attitude: 'Tout membre
de la classe dominante est homme de droit divin. Né dans un
milieu de chefs, il est persuadé dès son enfance qu'il est né *pour*
commander et, en un certain sens, cela est vrai puisque ses
parents, qui commandent, l'ont engendré pour qu'il prenne leur
suite... Attendu par ses pairs, destiné à les relever en temps
voulu, il existe parce qu'il *a le droit* d'exister' (*11*, pp.184-85).

Of course, such necessity is relative to the social order. For his
existence to appear absolutely justified, the *chef* has to identify
totally with his social function: 'il y a une certaine fonction
sociale qui l'attend dans l'avenir, dans laquelle il se coulera dès
qu'il en aura l'âge et qui est comme la réalité métaphysique de
son individu' (*11*, p.184). He may even invoke religion in
support of his claim to exist by right, the 'droit divin' of the
earlier quotation evoking the divine right of kings, by which
absolute monarchs claimed to be God's representative on earth.

The myth of necessity is exploded by Roquentin's experience
of his own contingency. His feeling of superfluity is in direct
opposition to the bourgeois's sense of personal necessity.
Roquentin does not feel himself to be an essential part of
existence, but rather that he is 'de trop' (p.181), something extra
that could easily be dispensed with. Both his personal existence
and the existence of the world are unjustifiable, and for the same
reason: neither is necessitated by God. However much the man-
made structures of the social order necessitate each other,

resembling in that the properties of a circle or a right-angled parallelepiped, nothing necessitates the fact that, unlike mathematical figures, the social order exists. Since the social order was not the result of a divine plan, no place in it was earmarked for Roquentin; no role awaited him at birth, neither will a gap be left by his death. Nowhere is he more conscious of this fact than in the museum, as he stands before the portraits of Bouville's past leaders: 'je n'avais pas le droit d'exister. J'étais apparu par hasard, j'existais comme une pierre, une plante, un microbe' (p.122). To believe otherwise would be to join forces with the 'salauds' (p.135), whom Sartre defines in *L'Existentialisme est un humanisme* as those 'qui essaieront de montrer que leur existence était nécessaire, alors qu'elle est la contingence même de l'apparition de l'homme sur la terre' (*8*, pp.84-85).

Identity and the social image

Because consciousness is not thinglike, introspection cannot produce a sense of identity. This can only come about through the mediation of others, for whom we exist as objects in the world. As Roquentin observes: 'Les gens qui vivent en société ont appris à se voir, dans les glaces, tels qu'ils apparaissent à leurs amis' (p.34). The spirit of seriousness inclines the bourgeois to regard this objective identity as the only significant dimension of human reality. It is because the bourgeois finds his reality in the eyes of others and in his social role that the Sunday-morning parade in the rue Tournebride assumes such importance. Being the preserve of the middle classes, the street provides a re-affirmation of class identity. It is for this reason that the young draughtsman is felt by one of the 'messieurs bien' to be trespassing (p.71).

Another illustration of the bourgeois belief in the essentially objective character of human reality is provided by the encounter between Dr Rogé and M. Achille on Mardi Gras. This time the objectivisation takes place not on the public, social level but on the private, psychological level. Just as the bourgeois is absorbed by his social class, so, under the ordering eye of Rogé, Achille's individuality is assimilated by the psychological class to which he is supposed by Rogé to belong: 'M. Achille est un cas, tout simplement, qui se laisse aisément ramener à quelques notions communes' (p.100). Rogé is guilty of putting the cart before the horse, of putting essences before existence. He sees Achille as a person with a recognisable psychological make-up, a character which is indistinguishable from that of other individuals of the same type. By sacrificing the particular to the general in this way, Rogé is discounting the individual as a unique, indivisible totality and as a free subject.

The same tendency to press human experience into the mould of essences is evident on a much grander scale in the false humanism of the Autodidacte. His indiscriminate love of mankind implies that all men are worthy of respect by virtue of the fact that they partake of the inherently noble nature of humanity. As Roquentin mockingly remarks: 'tous les hommes sont admirables... En tant que créatures de Dieu, naturellement' (p.170). Not only is the Autodidacte's love suspect by its universality but also it rests on the assumption, mistaken according to Sartre, that human nature is pre-defined. For the Catholic humanist, man, as a created object, corresponds to a concept in the mind of God, just as a paper-knife corresponds to an idea in the mind of the industrialist: 'l'homme individuel réalise un certain concept qui est dans l'entendement divin' (*8*, p.20).

Again it is Roquentin's own experience which gives the lie to this assumption. By the time he decides to leave Bouville, Roquentin feels devoid of any sense of social or psychic identity: 'Tout ce qui reste de réel, en moi, c'est de l'existence qui se sent exister' (p.236). More radically still, he comes close to losing his human identity altogether. Even as he leaves the restaurant where he has, ironically, been discussing humanism with the Autodidacte, he imagines himself to be seen by the other customers as 'un crabe qui s'échappait à reculons de cette salle si humaine' (p.174). This sense of otherness still haunts him when he stands on the hilltop overlooking Bouville: 'Il me semble que j'appartiens à une autre espèce' (p.220). The scene ends with a contemptuous dismissal of the notion of human dignity inherent in the humanist outlook: 'Qu'avez-vous fait de votre humanisme? Où est votre dignité de roseau pensant?' (p.223).

Sartre's point is that humanness is not something we are born with, but something acquired through learning and sustained by social intercourse.

Whether the bourgeois is defining himself in terms of social class or imposing definitions on others, he is guilty of suppressing an important truth about human beings: their freedom. Rogé's need to pigeon-hole others is symptomatic of the uneasiness we may feel when confronted by the other as a free subject. As Sartre observes in *L'Etre et le néant*: 'Qui ne voit, en effet, ce qu'il y a d'offensant pour autrui et de rassurant pour moi, dans une phrase comme: "Bah! c'est un pédéraste"' (*6*, p.105). The difference *Chez Camille* is that a sense of relief is felt by both labeller and labelled. Our own freedom can be as difficult to accept as that of others, in that it places responsibility for our actions squarely on our own shoulders. Consequently, belief in the objectivity of human reality is a comforting illusion. It makes life easier to believe that what we do is largely the result of what we are. Similarly, the old ladies of the Cour des Hypothèques find it easier to rely on traditional values rather than make the effort of thinking for themselves. Again Sartre has a word for such people: '[ceux] qui se cacheront, par l'esprit de sérieux ou par des excuses déterministes leur liberté totale, je les appellerai lâches' (*8*, p.84).

Ethics and the social norm

In *L'Existentialisme est un humanisme* Sartre maintains that the objectivity of values is dependent on the existence of God whom he dismisses as a logical impossibility: 'L'existentialiste... pense qu'il est très gênant que Dieu n'existe pas, car avec lui disparaît toute possibilité de trouver des valeurs dans un ciel intelligible; il ne peut plus y avoir de bien *a priori*, puisqu'il n'y a pas de conscience infinie et parfaite pour le penser' (*8*, pp.35-36). It is, of course, in the religious sphere that the notion of objective values can be most easily appreciated. The Old Testament provides a vivid illustration of objective values in the form of the stone tablets upon which were inscribed the Ten Commandments. Predictably, in *La Nausée* itself, bourgeois values are portrayed as having a strictly objective form. The old ladies of the Cour des Hypothèques have inherited their values, 'les saintes idées, les bonnes idées' (p.47), from their fathers. These values have, like all the other family heirlooms, been handed down through the generations. Although the father and grandfather have replaced God the Father, the essential point is that such values, having their origin in the past, are pre-established; already given, they have merely to be received by each individual.

This belief in inviolable, objective standards leads to the formation of a strongly paternalistic social structure which will ensure their preservation. Not surprisingly, Sartre devotes more attention to the figure of authority than to the willing victim, for the bourgeoisie is, as Blévigne reminds us, 'la classe dirigeante' (p.132). The subjects of the portraits which attract Roquentin's attention during his visit to the public gallery are prominent figures in the major areas of public life: Pacôme, the business-man, Rémy Parrottin, the university teacher, Jean Parrottin, the industrialist, and Olivier Blévigne, the politician. It is this unholy trinity of *pédagogue*, *patron* and *politicien* which is the butt of Sartre's satire. Just as the leader justifies his existence in the light of the job to be done, so he justifies his position of authority over others by invoking the idea of duty. For Pacôme, 'un droit n'est jamais que l'autre aspect d'un devoir' (p.123). Rights are not unfairly arrogated privileges but the natural con-sequence of obligations arising out of *a priori* values. For Blévigne, 'commander n'est pas un droit de l'élite; c'est son principal devoir' (p.132). Leadership is an obligation for the élite because God has assigned it to lead.

Finally, the *chef* has his counterpart on the family level in the person of the father or the grandfather. The grandfather derives his authority from age alone. The bourgeois mentality is past-orientated and the grandfather is the family's link with the past. But more importantly, the grandfather is, by virtue of his years, a man of experience, and experience is a qualification for leader-ship (p.132). Experience is singled out for special treatment by Sartre in the episode involving Dr Rogé, who regards Achille as no different from all the other 'vieux toqués' he has come

across. Roquentin compares him to those historians who
similarly oversimplify reality by reducing Lenin, Robespierre
and Cromwell to essentially the same type (p.102). In other
words, to have faith in experience is to believe that the present
can be explained in terms of the past, and consequently to be
blind to historical change and to the differences between
individuals. Sartre is sceptical of the value of these empirical
generalities. It goes without saying that he is equally scathing
about the further tendency of the bourgeois unconsciously to re-
interpret such generalities as prior essences.

Although Sartre's portrayal of the bourgeoisie in *La Nausée*
brings to light such stock failings as hypocrisy, self-interest and
self-importance, this is incidental to his main purpose of
exposing the ontological illusion underlying bourgeois morality.
As Sartre makes clear in *L'Existentialisme est un humanisme*, he
is attacking the bourgeoisie on grounds of authenticity rather
than of reference to moral standards: 'lâches ou salauds ne
peuvent être jugés que sur le plan de la stricte authenticité'
(p.85). And authenticity consists in living in conformity with the
human condition as existence. It is the supporting philosophical
framework that gives Sartre's critique its originality and distinguishes it from the social criticism of Flaubert or Balzac.

3. Existence and Art

For much of its duration, *La Nausée* hardly distinguishes between consciousness and material reality. After Roquentin's abandonment of his biography, however, there is a change of emphasis. The park episode provides us with a description of specifically non-human existence, which Sartre calls the *en-soi*. Roquentin is now made to feel that he is more than just bodily existence and that human reality, the *pour-soi* in Sartrean terminology, is essentially a transcending of its contingency as body. Another important contrast is that between existence and art. From the outset, art, in the form of the jazz song *Some of These Days* which Roquentin hears at frequent intervals during the novel, provides an antidote to his nausea. The song will make him increasingly aware of the differences between existent objects and aesthetic objects, which he will finally discover to be mutually exclusive. The discovery engenders a hope that artistic creation will, to some extent, redeem his existence.

L'Etre-en-soi

Through his experience of the tree-root in the park, Roquentin approaches an ideal limit, at which consciousness reveals being without in any way transforming it. The experience thus disposes of what Sartre believes to be the myth of an ordered external reality. Chapter One showed that certain, essentially social structures are not preordained but superimposed on being by consciousness. The revelation of existence presupposes that these ordering structures be neutralised, for its apprehension is an intuition and not the result of a process of reasoning: 'l'existence n'est pas quelque chose qui se laisse penser de loin: il faut que ça vous envahisse brusquement' (p.186). The 'marronnier' experience itself is 'une illumination', 'un dévoilement' (p.179). In his written account of the experience, Roquentin traces the progressive destructuring of existence which constitutes this 'unveiling' of its materiality. The destructuring process, which begins the moment Roquentin enters the park, comprises two main stages, each involving a facet of the 'figure-ground' experience characteristic of normal perception. The 'figure-ground' experience was first demonstrated by the Gestalt school, a group of German psychologists whose work was of particular interest to Sartre (*20*, pp.40-46). We perceive an object by making it stand out as a figure against a background, just as the words you are reading stand out against the whiteness of the page, despite the fact that the ink and the page are both on the same plane. Sartre uses this as evidence for the nihilating activity of consciousness: a tree appears to us as a tree to the extent that it is not everything else.

The first stage of the destructuring process is effected by the state of fascination induced in Roquentin through his contemplation of the tree-root. Chapter One showed how consciousness normally transcends its object, moving beyond it in a flight towards its own possibility and the object's potential. In fascination, consciousness is bound to its object. It is the overwhelming proximity of himself to objects which Roquentin first notes in the diary entry. Existence invades his senses: 'le marronnier se pressait contre mes yeux' (p.180). Later on, when the word 'fascination' makes its appearance in the text, the lack of distance between consciousness and its object becomes a quasi-fusion: '*J'étais* la racine de marronnier... perdu en elle, rien d'autre qu'elle' (p.185). Now the appearance of objects as instruments depends on their being figured in a world organised as a 'complexe d'ustensilité' and serving as ground: I am sitting on a chair which is close to a desk which supports my paper on which I am writing with a pen, etc. But when a consciousness becomes fascinated, a single object is lifted out of its ground and focused in its 'être-lá' character, such that it is no longer seen as a 'chose-ustensile', but as a 'chose existante': 'Dans la fascination il n'y a plus rien qu'un objet géant dans un monde désert' (*6*, p.226). In isolating an object in this way, fascination destructures the 'outer horizon' of that object: Roquentin no longer sees the root in terms of its identity, in terms of its relation to and distinctness from other objects, but in terms of its qualities.

Normally, an individual object is perceived as a synthetic unity of qualities, one or more of which are figured against others which fall into a 'ground' function. For example, the woolliness of a red rug interpenetrates with its redness; yet we see the rug as a redness which is woolly *or* as a woolliness which is red. In other words, the way in which the 'figure-ground' relation operates to organise our perception of an object's qualities is similar to the way in which it operates to figure the object as a whole against the background 'complexe d'ustensilité' or 'world'. The second stage in the destructuring process is reached when this hierarchical ordering of an object's qualities, the object's 'inner horizon', is also obliterated. The root's qualities now appear all on the same level. As a result, each one is not the quality of a thing, as it is when structured in the 'figure-ground' relation, but itself becomes a thing, a piece of being: 'Chacune de ses qualités lui échappait un peu, coulait hors d'elle, se solidifiait à demi, devenait presque une chose; chacune était *de trop dans* la racine, et la souche tout entière me donnait à présent l'impression de rouler un peu hors d'elle-même, de se nier, de se perdre dans un étrange excès' (p.183).

The destructuring of the root's 'inner horizon' becomes more obvious when Roquentin attempts to focus his attention on a single quality: the root's colour. The blackness stands out only momentarily, quickly losing its prominence and thus its uniqueness as a quality: 'ça *ressemblait* à une couleur mais aussi... ça se fondait... en odeur noire... Je ne le *voyais* pas simplement ce noir: la vue, c'est une invention abstraite, une idée nettoyée, simplifiée, une idée d'homme. Ce noir-là, présence amorphe et veule, débordait, de loin, la vue, l'odorat et le goût. Mais cette richesse tournait en confusion et finalement ça n'était plus rien parce que c'était trop' (p.184). The qualities of the root, having lost their hierarchical structure, bombard Roquentin's senses simultaneously. The root now appears as being, because it is quality, as distinct from objects, which reveals being, and because, in being, every quality pervades every other: 'le citron est étendu tout à travers ses qualités et chacune de ses qualités est

étendue tout à travers chacune des autres' (6, p.235). There is a
third stage to Roquentin's experience of existence. Not only is
the root isolated from other objects and reduced to a collection
of qualities, but the qualities of being are reduced to a single
quality: Roquentin ultimately sees existence as a sticky, homo-
geneous paste. But this stage belongs to the novel's psychological dimension and will be discussed in the next chapter.

The failure of Roquentin's consciousness to structure
existence causes him to experience it as 'too much'. A key-word
in his communication of the feeling of over-abundance is
'déborder', which occurs four times in the diary entry, though
with different nuances of meaning. In Sartre's philosophy, the
'débordement' of objects is intuitive evidence of their
contingency. By 'débordement', Sartre means that material
objects 'overflow' what we perceive of them and therefore the
concepts within which we try to encapsulate them. The blackness
of the tree root, being the blackness of an existent object, is
inexhaustible, it overflows the concept of blackness. Such
richness defies Roquentin's attempt to reduce the root to conceptual thought and underlines the impossibility of rationalising
existence. To make his meaning clearer, Roquentin compares
the tree-root with a circle, which is an ideal object. Ideal objects
are, by definition, non-existent. Whether circles are drawn in ink
or chalk does not impinge upon their circularity. Because
existence is not part of their definition, they can be fully
described and are thus fully intelligible. If existence were a
property of a circle, the latter could never be fully defined
because the reality of an object is inexhaustible, consisting as it
does for Sartre of the synthetic totality of its appearances, which
are infinite: 'Cette racine... existait dans la mesure où je ne
pouvais pas l'expliquer' (p.182).

Roquentin ends the first part of his description of existence on
a more traditionally philosophical note, by opposing contingency to necessity. These two categories apply to two areas of
being, the material and the ideal, which are mutually exclusive.
Necessity can never be a property of the former: 'le monde des
explications et des raisons n'est pas celui de l'existence' (p.182),
whereas 'exister, c'est *être là*, simplement; les existants

apparaissent, se laissent *rencontrer*, mais on ne peut jamais les *déduire*' (pp.184-85). The significance of the contrast between 'rencontrer' and 'déduire' is perhaps most clearly brought out if we compare the method of the experimental sciences with that of purely formal disciplines like mathematics and logic. The latter are the province of deductive reasoning, the steps of which are necessary. In logic, for example, the conclusion of a syllogism will of necessity follow from its premises. The premises and conclusion are unaffected by what does or does not exist, and the transition from the first to the second explicates purely formal relations between propositions. The laws of science, on the other hand, lack the necessity of the *a priori* laws of deductive reason. The method of science is mainly inductive, its laws are based on empirical data, which are encountered ('rencontrés') and which may at any time be invalidated by new data. Existence is 'sans raison, sans cause et sans nécessité' (*6*, p.713). Roquentin more than once asserts that existence is an absolute. Sartre will argue the same point in *L'Etre et le néant*: 'l'en-soi lui-même n'a pas besoin de pour-soi pour être' (*6*, p.716). This is because only the *pour-soi* and the *en-soi* exist, and the former is essentially a negation of the latter. Consequently, 'la conscience envisagée à part n'est qu'une abstraction' (*6*, p.716). Roquentin puts it more familiarly: 'pour imaginer le néant, il fallait qu'on se trouve déjà là, en plein monde et les yeux grands ouverts et vivant; le néant ça n'était qu'une idée dans ma tête, une idée existante' (p.189).

Roquentin makes one more discovery about existence: it is plenitude or actuality — an absence of potentiality which opposes it to consciousness, the latter being conceived by Sartre as a lack and as possibility. The restrictive features presented by being-in-itself do not belong to it, but are projected on to it by consciousness: 'c'est par la réalité humaine que le *manque* vient aux choses sous forme de "puissance", "d'inachèvement", de "sursis", de "potentialité"' (*6*, p.246). A crescent moon, to take one of Sartre's own examples, may be perceived either as a phase (restriction) of the full moon or simply as a fully actual crescent shape in the sky. In the former case, the crescent moon is transcended towards the future by a consciousness which relates it to an as yet unrealised full moon. It is only in the light of this human transcendence that the crescent moon acquires its restriction and the potentiality of becoming a full moon. If the crescent moon is not transcended, 'il se dévoile comme étant pleinement ce qu'il est, ce signe concret dans le ciel, qui n'a besoin de rien pour être ce qu'il est' (*6*, p.246). In other words, the crescent moon itself may equally well appear as a fullness, in which case it will no more be perceived as a full moon with a large piece missing than a Café Mably croissant would appear as a once round bun with a large bite taken out of it.

Freed from his fascination with the root, Roquentin notices that the top of the tree has begun to sway in the wind. He first interprets the movement as a 'passage à l'existence' (p.186), as if nature had the power to create: 'Je m'apprêtais à les [= les mouvements] voir sortir du néant' (p.186). He quickly realises, however, that the movement is no more than the coming together of two, already existent, physical phenomena. He had mistakenly assumed that the movement had been generated by a potentiality of the tree. But potentiality is a feature only of the human world; in nature there is only actuality: 'Tout était plein, tout en acte' (p.187).

L'Etre-pour-soi

For Sartre the terms 'human reality', 'pour-soi', 'consciousness' are interchangeable. He holds that a human being is essentially a consciousness, which in its primary form is not linked to a self but is pure awareness. As such, consciousness is a lack: 'la réalité humaine est avant tout son propre néant' (*6*, p.132). It is for this reason that human beings have potentiality whereas things do not. Human beings, according to Sartre, 'make themselves' by realising their possibilities which, by definition, do not exist. Consciousness as lack needs an object in order to exist at all. Having no substance of its own, it 'borrows' its being from its object, defining itself negatively in terms of that object: '[elle] se fait qualifier *dehors* auprès d'un certain être comme *n'étant pas* cet être; c'est précisément ce qu'on appelle: être conscience *de* quelque chose' (*6*, p.223).

Any act of consciousness, the perception of a table, for

example, entails the nihilation of its object: to look at a table is for consciousness to be aware of itself as *not* the table, not as something positive apart from the table; the perceiving is not done by an 'I' but by a pure consciousness. Now while most of us would readily concur that we are aware of not being the table we are looking at, rather fewer of us would concede that there is no 'I' doing the looking. For the common-sense view would be that there are a 'self' and a table separated by a spatial distance. The reason for this misconception, as Sartre would call it, is that consciousness is located in space by virtue of being tied to a body, and there is clearly a physical distance between body and table. However, the distance implied by Sartre's reference to the object as being *outside* consciousness is not a physical one. Physical distance would not affect the fundamental structure of my conscious relation to the table. That relation would be no differently one of nihilation if, instead of sitting at the table, I were standing ten feet away from it or, for that matter, on holiday in Sydney; except that in this last case my consciousness would no longer be a perceiving consciousness but an imagining one. 'Distance' is really a metaphor for the non-spatial dissociation effected by nihilation. Indeed, because all that nihilation interposes between consciousness and its object is a dissociating 'nothing' rather than the act of a Cartesian thinking substance, the distance between consciousness and its object could be described as a separation without distance.

The purest example of the relation between being and consciousness is the state of fascination, which Sartre describes at some length in *L'Etre et le néant*: 'Dans ces cas, en effet, qui représentent le fait immédiat du connaître, le connaissant n'est absolument rien qu'une pure négation, il ne se trouve ni ne se récupère nulle part, il *n'est pas*; la seule qualification qu'il puisse supporter, c'est qu'il *n'est pas*, précisément, tel objet fascinant' (*6*, p.226). Fascination, then, exemplifies the negativity of consciousness because the latter fails to project itself beyond the object towards its own possibilities. Roquentin's own account of fascination appears at first sight to contradict this description, but only because the relation receives a different emphasis in *La Nausée*: '*J'étais* la racine de marronnier. Ou plutôt j'étais tout

entier conscience de son existence. Encore détaché d'elle —
puisque j'en avais conscience — et pourtant perdu en elle, rien
d'autre qu'elle' (p.185). Roquentin's account stresses the
immediacy of his intuition of existence as undifferentiated
fullness. In the extract from *L'Etre et le néant*, however, the
emphasis is on the pure negativity of consciousness: there is
never a total fusion between consciousness and its object, not
even in fascination. This shift of emphasis in the philosophical
work is reflected syntactically by the relegation to a subordinate
clause of the statement concerning the intuitive nature of true
knowledge.

Since Roquentin is a fictional character and not a professional
philosopher, he must be made to feel the nothingness of consciousness and not to demonstrate it rationally. Roquentin's
reunion with Anny, the subject of the next substantial diary
entry after the park episode, provides the pretext. The meeting
itself already begins to undermine the notion of a permanent
self, since each attempts, and fails, to find in the other the
partner of former days. The prospect of a definitive break with
Anny accelerates the process of dissolution of the self. After
taking his leave of Anny, Roquentin feels utterly abandoned and
that he no longer exists for anyone: 'elle s'est vidée de moi d'un
coup et toutes les autres consciences du monde sont, elles aussi,
vides de moi' (p.236). Now, as we saw in Chapter One, it is
chiefly through others that we acquire a sense of self, because
the look of the other objectifies us. His links now severed with
Anny, the Autodidacte and Bouville itself, Roquentin's
depersonalisation becomes complete: 'Et soudain le Je pâlit,
pâlit et c'en est fait, il s'éteint' (p.236). In the next paragraph,
the loss of self is expressed linguistically by the substitution of
the impersonal locution 'il y a conscience' for the personal
pronoun 'je'.

Roquentin has thus acquired a Sartrean insight into the
essence of consciousness. When he speaks of his now
anonymous consciousness as 'une petite transparence vivante et
impersonnelle' (p.237), he is echoing the thesis of *La
Transcendance de l'Ego* (4), which Sartre resumes thus: 'l'Ego
apparaît à la conscience comme un en-soi transcendant, comme

un existant du monde humain, non comme *de la* conscience' (*6*, p.147). In other words, the self is a product or an object of reflective consciousness and not a conscious subject or the source of consciousness. If primary consciousness were personal it would possess a degree of opacity, and thereby lose the transparency experienced by Roquentin and considered by Sartre as a *sine qua non* of consciousness. Consciousness must, by definition, be conscious of itself. Sartre is careful, however, to distinguish between this kind of self-consciousness and the more orthodox reflective kind which is consciousness of a *self*. Roquentin's words spell this out: the self-consciousness in question is a 'conscience hélas! de la conscience' (p.238). Sartre does not, of course, deny the existence of the self. And Roquentin himself regains his sense of identity as he approaches the café: 'Voilà le *Rendez-vous des Cheminots* et le Moi jaillit dans la conscience, c'est *moi*, Antoine Roquentin, je pars pour Paris tout à l'heure; je viens faire mes adieux à la patronne' (p.239). What happens here is that Roquentin *first of all* becomes conscious of the café he is approaching. He *then*, through an act of reflection, posits his non-reflective awareness of the café as being a project to go and say goodbye to the *patronne*.

Art

The editors of the Pléiade edition of Sartre's novels inform us that Sartre's own thoughts on contingency were prompted, like Roquentin's, by the differences between real life and art: 'Sartre lui-même a plusieurs fois affirmé que ses premières idées sur la contingence furent suggérées par la comparaison entre l'impression de nécessité produite par les images d'un film et le sentiment de gratuité absurde que donne l'écoulement de la vie réelle' (*3*, p.1661). In Roquentin's case, of course, it is literature and music, and not the cinema, which promote his insight. Nevertheless, the particular qualities of the song which appeal to Roquentin are shared by other aesthetic objects: its non-existence and the aesthetic or felt necessity of its unreal temporal structure. It will be useful, therefore, before turning to the role played by music and literature in *La Nausée*, to start with a brief account of Sartre's views on the nature of art in general, which are related to his theory of the imagination.

In *L'Imaginaire*, a work which was published two years after *La Nausée*, Sartre argues that the capacity to imagine is intrinsic to consciousness. Now, as we saw earlier in this chapter, an act of consciousness involves a transcending of its object. The latter thereby acquires the negative quality of 'having been gone beyond' towards the real world as a whole. Similarly, in imagining, consciousness goes beyond, not just a single object, but the real world as a whole. The real world is posited as *lacking* an imaged object which, at the same time, is posited outside it as *not* belonging to it. The essential difference between the functions of the nihilating transcendence in either case is this: in imagining we transcend the whole of reality towards an unreal object, whereas in perceiving we transcend a particular real 'ceci' towards the whole of the real world, to appropriate which is always the fundamental meaning of every conscious project. In perceiving we remain within the world. In imagining we posit an object outside the world, *yet which remains essentially relative to it*, just as a shadow depends for its existence on the ground on which it falls. Sartre was later to declare that his conception of the imaginary changed between *La Nausée* and *L'Imaginaire* (*14*, p.59), the essential difference being that in the novel the imaginary is treated as an autonomous realm, a second world, whereas in his study of the imagination Sartre states that 'il n'y a pas de monde irréel' (*5*, p.171). The imaginary is now seen as a kind of shadow-show dependent on the real, a conception which adds weight to the suspicion that the escape into art is illusory as well as morally reprehensible.

Each time he hears the tune *Some of These Days*, Roquentin is struck by the fact that it does not share the defects of existent objects: 'elle n'a rien de trop' (p.243). An imaginary object, unlike a perceived object which, as we saw earlier in the chapter, 'overflows' our consciousness of it, is characterised by 'une espèce de pauvreté essentielle' (*5*, p.20). In other words, we never discover in it more than we ourselves put into it. The tune is not even influenced by things that exist: '*Elle* n'existe pas... si je me levais, si j'arrachais ce disque du plateau qui le supporte et si je le cassais en deux, je ne l'atteindrais pas, *elle*. Elle est au-delà — toujours au-delà de quelque chose, d'une voix, d'une note de violon... Elle *est*' (p.243). One accepts without difficulty that the song is distinct from the record. But in what sense is it different from the notes played? *L'Imaginaire* provides the answer.

Sartre's argument will emerge more clearly if we start with the example he takes from painting. If we look at a portrait of Charles VIII, we may choose to see it as a material object, as an object which *exists*. In this case our consciousness aims at the materials with which the artist has worked and the frame. When we experience the painting as a work of art, on the other hand, the material object gives way to an imaginary object, an object which, in Roquentin's terms, simply *is*. This object is neither the materiality of the portrait nor the real Charles VIII, but an unreal image of a once real king. The material, 'face-like' object is not the aesthetic object; it is simply the support or sensory material by means of which the imagining consciousness consti-tutes a wholly immaterial work of art that is quite distinct from it. Sartre calls this material support an 'analogon'. In the same way, the performance of a piece of music is nothing more than the 'analogon' of the work itself; the notes, taken at their face value, being pure sound, just as the paint on the canvas or wood is pure colour.

Roquentin is attracted not merely by the absence from the song of the physical properties of existent objects, but, more positively, by the song's formal qualities. An essential feature of his aesthetic experiences is a sense of inevitable progression. The song, story-telling and his own 'adventures' are all characterised by the same necessity. He describes all three in a way which cuts across the divisions between them. The singer's voice, for instance, is an 'événement': 'Quelques secondes encore et la Négresse va chanter... Si j'aime cette belle voix, c'est surtout pour ça... elle est l'événement que tant de notes ont préparé' (p.39). Similarly, the beginning of an adventure is compared to 'une sonnerie de trompette' (p.60), with the adventure becoming, on its completion, 'cette belle forme mélodique' (p.60). The progression in question is a temporal rather than a logical one. Indeed, the difference between real-life time and the time of literature and music will be the most important factor in the contrast between art and existence.

According to Sartre, time is not an *a priori* dimension of existence into which a consciousness is subsequently inserted, but is introduced into existence by consciousness itself. When he says that being-in-itself is what it is, the tense is significant: being is; it is neither what it was nor what it will be. Consciousness, on the other hand, '[est] ce qu'il n'est pas et n'[est] pas ce qu'il est' (*6*, p.33). In other words, consciousness lacks being; it is its own possibilities, which are, by definition, future. Time is precisely this self-projection of consciousness towards a future possibility. This is why time stops, when Roquentin's consciousness fails to transcend the tree-root (p.185). Sartre's handling of time in *La Nausée* is extremely subtle. Three different kinds of time are involved: the time of real life as normally experienced, which is a progression; Roquentin's time, which is not a progression but an accumulation; and the ideal time of the temporal arts, which is a necessary progression.

When we are actually living 'in' time, we do not experience it as a divisible totality. We do not pass through it as though it were a tunnel in which our consciousness is, at any given moment, at a point between two ends. In living, we project ourselves towards the future, from which we are separated by the non-spatial, therefore indivisible, 'distance' of the kind already discussed. In addition, the future is never reached but constantly recedes. As soon as it is made present, it is replaced by another future, so that we never have the impression of a clear-cut ending. A definitive totality will not be realised until our death, and so we cannot know the relation of any single project to it. As for the past, it comes into existence as 'that which has been gone beyond': for Sartre, 'le passé' is 'le dépassé' (*6*, p.184).

As well as living through time, we can also watch it pass; by observing, for instance, the movement of the hands of a clock. The perspective then changes and time becomes divisible into a series of instants. If we reflect on time that has already passed, another radical change of perspective becomes possible. Time now acquires a closed form; events, our past experiences, viewed in retrospect, are capable of being given a recognisable beginning and end. Moreover, in retelling our experiences, we confer on them a sense of unity and progression, seeing each part in relation to the whole. The reason is that 'les événements se produisent dans un sens et nous les racontons en sens inverse' (p.63). Story-telling is the art of making everything look as if it points to a conclusion from the start, particularly if the story-teller omits all digressions from the retelling.

Roquentin's own experience of time is, predictably, abnormal. It is a pool which spreads slowly outwards, a 'flaque visqueuse' (p.38), a 'mare noire' (p.185). It does not move forward because Roquentin's consciousness frequently fails to transcend the present instant towards the future. His time is the projectless time of inactivity or boredom. When he tries to observe time passing, either it appears not to pass at all, an impression he illustrates through the imperceptibility of the ageing process (p.85), or else it is nothing more than an ever-renewed present, which may be compared to the repetitive ticking of a handless clock, the seconds of which pile up instead of leading somewhere. Roquentin's time is a deposited or a secreted time rather than a time which generates a future yet to be realised. Even when he does see time as linear, its progress is a sluggish, halting one, as when he watches an old woman walk along the street (p.51). In this instance, time appears to pass with painful slowness because Roquentin's consciousness, functioning normally for once, transcends her actual position in the street, thereby plotting her course in advance. Another peculiarity of Roquentin's time is that it is never-ending as well as accumulative, it is an 'addition interminable' (p.62). This is because he no longer gives a closed form to his past experiences by recounting them to others (p.20); neither does he give a direction to his future, since his life is so aimless that nothing special ever needs to be done. As a result, time appears to him as an ever-expanding bag: 'le temps est trop large, il ne se laisse pas remplir' (pp.37-38). Herein lies an important difference between real life and the sense of adventure he occasionally experiences: in real life, 'on a l'impression qu'on peut faire ce qu'on veut, aller de l'avant ou revenir en arrière, que ça n'a pas d'importance' (p.86); whereas in an adventure, 'il ne s'agit pas de manquer son coup parce qu'on ne pourrait plus le recommencer' (p.86).

We have seen that, in recounting our experiences, we shape them, by relating every detail to the outcome. The word 'raconter', of course, as readily evokes fiction as it does real-life experiences, and the novelist, even more obviously, shapes his material with the end of his novel in mind. Sartre once said of *La Nausée* itself that the aesthetic solution envisaged by Roquentin was 'le point de départ, l'idée première de la chose' (*14*, p.59). As Roquentin himself says about stories, true and fictional, 'la fin est là qui transforme tout' (p.63). For the reader, who does not possess the novelist's omniscience, the novel is only progressively realised. Nevertheless, he senses that it is moving unerringly towards an ending which, in retrospect, will be confirmed as a necessary one, and not one of several possible endings. The necessity in question is not, however, the causal necessity of determinism, the push from behind, as it were, to which material things are passively subjected. The necessity of adventures and of the song is a future-orientated one. The emphasis is on the present instant or note as generating what is to come and not on the present as issuing mechanically from what has gone before: 'chaque instant ne paraît que pour amener ceux qui suivent' (p.60). The instants form not only a whole but a dynamic whole, each calling forth the subsequent instants as that which is necessary to complete the totality: 'ils sont happés par la fin de l'histoire qui les attire' (p.63). It is for this reason that the necessity in question is temporal rather than logical. It is an ideal time which Roquentin's consciousness seeks to reproduce in real life through adventures.

Not only Roquentin but Anny, too, tries to convert real time into the time of art. Whenever they met during their stay in the Middle East, Anny would, by isolating the last hour of their day together, confer on 'lived' time the closed form of narrative time. The imposition of a beginning and end made time appear both more precious and more visible, since it was then experienced as progressing towards a point: 'A partir de cet instant, nous commençâmes à sentir couler les minutes' (p.86). As for Roquentin, he experiences the time of his adventures not merely as a progression, but as a necessary progression. This necessity allows him to live through an event as if it were a work of art. During an adventure, he is 'heureux comme un héros de roman' (p.82). His Sunday adventure causes him to experience each moment as part of a necessary sequence, in opposition to the contingently connected moments of real life. Each of his gestures becomes irrevocable: 'le moindre geste m'engage' (p.83) and he moves forward 'avec le sentiment de la fatalité' (p.82). When the adventure is completed, its formal unity is fully realised and appreciated: 'Du fond de ce café quelque chose revient en arrière sur les moments épars de ce dimanche et les soude les uns aux autres, leur donne un sens' (p.84). Roquentin's adventures are, then, no ordinary adventures. It is not an exciting content which defines them but their aesthetic necessity. The point is underlined by the unexciting setting Sartre has chosen for the one adventure in the novel: not even the combined talents of a Fleming and a Forsythe could have turned a Bouville Sunday into a box-office bonanza.

Roquentin's adventures provide him, therefore, with an insight into temporality as Sartre conceives it. His experience of time is, however, a rather special one. In Sartrean philosophy, the time of real life is closer to the time of art than Roquentin would have us believe. The time of the refrain in *La Nausée*, which 'se jette en avant', becomes, in *L'Etre et le néant*, the time of normal consciousness as 'projet'. In fact, Sartre more than once uses this phrase in the latter work to describe the flight of consciousness towards its future. Moreover, *L'Etre et le néant* further assimilates art and conscious existence, when Sartre compares the unity of the work of art to the unity of a project: '... comme dans l'œuvre d'art, chaque structure partielle indique, de diverses manières, diverses autres structures partielles et la structure totale' (*6*, p.581). The difference between the two, for Sartre the philosopher, is that the unity of the work of art is a necessary unity, whereas a project is maintained in existence by the contingent act of continuing to choose

it. Sartre the novelist, however, creates a much bolder contrast
between real life and art as they relate to time. Roquentin's
experience of real-life time not only lacks necessity, it also lacks
a progression. Sartre is able to achieve this contrast without
betraying his philosophical position because Roquentin's time is
a projectless time; his consciousness has ceased to be a flight and
has become bogged down in existence.

Not the least of Sartre's achievements in *La Nausée* is to have
conveyed in a non-technical, literary register the complex ideas
resumed in the present chapter. Equally impressive, however, is
the thematic and stylistic coherence of the fictional world itself.
Sartre's skill as a novelist is already evident in his handling of
real-life time in the novel: it is consistent with the breakdown of
Roquentin's consciousness and reflects those qualities of
existence generally which most disgust Roquentin: real time in
La Nausée is inert, shapeless and wet. Consequently, the treatment of time both exemplifies the main opposition between
existence and art and at the same time strengthens the psychological motivation for the escape into art which Roquentin
ultimately contemplates. Sartre's philosophical novel is clearly
more than the ideas it contains. How much more will be the
subject of the next chapter.

4. *The Art of* La Nausée

Our evaluation of *La Nausée* as a work of literature will depend to a large extent on whether or not we feel that Sartre has succeeded in fusing its literary and philosophical elements. The main problem facing the writer who tries to combine literature and philosophy is that they are, in many respects, distinct domains. A major concern of the novelist is the concrete and the particular; his novel will be judged in part by the vividness with which it conveys the texture of real life. The philosopher, on the other hand, deals in general propositions and the logical relationships between them; and his work will be judged by the intellectual rigour of its arguments. Existentialism, however, has narrowed the gap between literature and philosophy, since it takes as its starting point human subjectivity which, for Sartre, is rooted in the real world. Existentialist philosophy, like literature, focuses on 'man in the world' and on 'things themselves'; on quite ordinary things, moreover, like paper-knives and Cousin Adolphe's braces. For traditional philosophy, the cup I see on the table in front of me is a purely material object of which the philosopher must ask whether it continues to exist when it is not being perceived. For Sartre, it is a 'chose-ustensile', something perceived originally as an instrument from the point of view of which consciousness is situated in a 'world of tasks'. It is no accident, therefore, that Sartre, like several of his contemporaries, should have been both a philosopher and a writer of fiction.

In her autobiography, Simone de Beauvoir alludes to this filiation between literature and existentialist philosophy in the case of *La Nausée* itself: '[Aux yeux de Sartre] la Contingence n'était pas une notion abstraite mais une dimension réelle du monde: il fallait utiliser toutes les ressources de l'art pour rendre sensible au cœur cette secrète "faiblesse" qu'il apercevait dans l'homme et dans les choses' (*16*, p.342). Her words underline the

difference between Sartre's approach to contingency and that of
his Anglo-Saxon contemporaries, for whom contingency is a
purely formal property of statements. For these philosophers,
statements of fact about the world, such as 'it is raining today',
are contingently true. Such philosophers take for granted what
Sartre is intent on revealing: the contingency of being. In 1972,
Sartre gave his own version of how he came to write *La Nausée*,
and although he viewed from a different angle from Beauvoir
the relationship between literature and philosophy in his novel,
he nevertheless reaffirmed the value of literature as a means of
communicating the intuition of contingency:

> on voit dans le roman *La Nausée* un personnage qui a
> effectivement une certaine forme d'intuition qu'on
> pourrait presque appeler pathologique, qui est la Nausée: il
> s'aperçoit de ce qu'est l'être et les créatures autour de lui.
> Mais je n'ai jamais eu à proprement parler cette 'nausée';
> c'est-à-dire que je la réclame quand même, mais beaucoup
> plus philosophique. C'était une certaine conception du
> monde en général et qui ne donnait pas lieu à des intuitions
> très particulières comme celle de la racine d'un arbre dans
> un jardin. [...] C'était plutôt des idées que j'avais — bien
> qu'en effet il y ait eu certains moments où j'ai vu les choses
> comme cela — qu'une impression constante comme a ce
> personnage. (*3*, p.1699)

Sartre's distinction between the literary experience of Roquentin
and his own philosophical experience gives some indication of
the gap that even an existentialist novelist must bridge between
literature and philosophy.

Claude-Edmonde Magny saw *La Nausée* as a 'compromis
entre la littérature et la philosophie' (*38*, p.168). Her judgement
draws attention to the difficulties which beset the philosopher-
novelist. If he is too preoccupied with the universal truths of
philosophy, then his novel will be too abstract. Magny feels that
La Nausée itself lacks the texture of real life: 'le livre cesse
presque d'être un roman, faute de rester suffisamment charnel;
il n'est plus qu'une expérience phénoménologique' (*38*, p.275).

She also feels that the novel fails as philosophy, because Roquentin is too idiosyncratic to be the bearer of a philosophical truth: '*La Nausée* tend à nous apparaître plus comme le journal d'un schizophrène que comme une révélation authentique sur le monde' (*38*, p.163). Sartre, having himself described Roquentin's experience as pathological, would not have entirely disagreed. He was caught in a vicious circle. His intention was to express through Roquentin a privileged insight into existence. But since privileged insights are, by definition, denied to most people, Roquentin had to be in some way exceptional for the experience to be motivated. The more exceptional he is made to appear, however, the more likely the reader is to attribute the insight to Roquentin's idiosyncrasies rather than to the way existence really is.

Consequently, another problem raised by philosophical literature is one faced by the reader: while the novelist's task is to disguise the philosophy in his novel by converting ideas into lived experience, the reader's problem is that of identifying and understanding the disguised philosophy. The average reader of *La Nausée* is easily misled into thinking that, for Sartre, human beings are no different from other species, language and science are of no use and nature is lawless and viscous. It is, then, extremely difficult at times to distinguish between what is peculiar to Roquentin's experience and what is generalisable from it. Nor is a thorough knowledge of Sartre's philosophy always a help, since *La Nausée* is more than a mere transposition of ideas which are systematised in the philosophical works. Occasionally, even seasoned *sartristes* fall into the trap of forcing the literature into the philosophical mould.

All this makes *La Nausée* a difficult work. But although I have used *L'Etre et le néant* to bring into sharper focus the novel's philosophical dimension, I would not want to imply that it is indispensable to our understanding of *La Nausée*. A close reading of the novel attests to a high degree of structural and stylistic coherence which is equally revelatory of the novel's meaning. Before turning to this aspect, however, let us first of all examine Magny's criticism.

Characterisation

A discussion of the characters of a novel written in the first person in which the narrator himself has no sense of personal identity and spends most of his time in the company of objects, or else with people he scarcely distinguishes from objects, may not appear very promising. It will, however, help us to decide whether Sartre has managed to reconcile the conflicting demands of fiction and philosophy.

Firstly, then, is Roquentin really no more than a vehicle for a philosophical demonstration? Magny herself, and more recently Geneviève Idt for whom Roquentin is 'non un moi qu'on pourrait décrire, mais une conscience vide toujours tournée vers le dehors' (*35*, p.61), have perhaps exaggerated his lack of individuality. Idt's description is not so much wrong as misleading: it invites us to regard Roquentin as a rather colourless figure, whereas in reality his irreverent humour alone does much to establish him as a character in the eyes of the reader: 'Dire qu'il y a des imbéciles pour puiser des consolations dans les beaux-arts. Comme ma tante Bigeois... les salles de concert regorgent d'humiliés, d'offensés qui, les yeux clos, cherchent à transformer leurs pâles visages en antennes réceptrices... Les cons' (p.242). The diary-format is well suited to the raciness and occasional coarseness of Roquentin's language and contributes stylistically to his self-portrait. There are other traits, too, such as his awkwardness in Anny's company or his exasperation with, but subsequent concern for, the Autodidacte, which help to individualise him. But most importantly, Roquentin has strong likes and dislikes, which confers on *La Nausée* an important psychological dimension.

The psychology in question is not, however, psychology of the traditional kind. The diary not only records a revelation of brute existence, it shows existence refracted by Roquentin's personal obsession: the world he sees is haunted by viscosity. The word itself occurs only once in the entire novel. But one of Roquentin's pet hates is mud; and at the climactic moment of revelation, the entire park, indeed the whole of existence, becomes for him 'une confiture', 'cette ignoble marmelade', an 'affalement gélatineux', a 'saleté poisseuse' (p.189). There is no suggestion, however, that the obsession is irreducibly subjective. It has, in fact, an ontological basis. Roquentin's intuition of brute existence first comes to him through an awareness of his own body, because it is through the body that one is, as it were, 'plugged into' material reality. Now, the human body is experienced by Roquentin as predominantly viscous, owing to its material composition and the spontaneous secretions which he finds so abhorrent. It is this equation of 'bodily' and 'viscous' which accounts for the obsession.

A consequence of the obsession is that objects, for Roquentin, fall into one of two distinct categories: either they evoke bodily existence and appear as repulsive or else, less frequently, they are seen as being far removed from organic life, in which case they appear as attractive. Roquentin's tendency to focus on the former gives rise to an exaggeratedly ugly picture of material reality. This does mean, as Magny suggests, that the psychological dimension is in danger of undermining the universal validity of Roquentin's experience. But again, Sartre avoids the suggestion of an eccentric personality, by giving Roquentin the kind of life-style conducive to such an obsession. Roquentin's solitary existence subjects him to a process of social deconditioning. Having neither family nor friends, he lacks the sense of personal identity that other people confer on us. He no longer needs to articulate his thoughts and feelings for the benefit of others. His thoughts are confined to the highly speculative reconstruction of the life of an eighteenth-century diplomat. To make matters worse, Roquentin has no roots, having spent much of his adult life travelling the world. The resulting lack of possessions deprives him both of a material expression of his personality and of the possibility of preserving his past by the association of certain objects with particular experiences. His activities as an amateur historian also play their part: the absence of a steady routine deprives him of the means by which other people mask the arbitrariness of their lives and his lack of social relevance exacerbates his sense of superfluity. A visit to the local art gallery, where he is confronted by the *chef*, the paradigm of integration, will be a major factor in his discovery of his absolute contingency. On the technical level, too, Sartre accelerates Roquentin's desocialisation, by causing him to see himself and other people from unusual angles or distances. It is this absence of psychological abnormality that warrants Idt's description of Roquentin as 'une conscience vide'.

As for the secondary characters, they offer further illustrations, in a non-bourgeois context, of the discrepancy between existence as it is in itself and human representations of it. The Autodidacte's 'appetite' for learning derives from the mistaken belief that the human mind is capable of converting material reality into mental substance. When he trots back to his seat in the library with his coveted volumes, he is compared to 'un chien qui a trouvé un os' (p.49). The image is particularly apt. On the purely behavioural level, it is both expressive and funny. Stylistically, it blends well with the general tendency of the imagery to break down the distinction between the human and the animal. Thematically, it pokes fun at those philosophical systems, disparagingly referred to by Sartre as 'philosophie alimentaire' (*9*, p.31), which held that reality could be assimilated in this way or, as Sartre himself puts it in the same essay, that 'connaître, c'est manger'. Implicit in Sartre's attack on science in the novel is his belief that knowledge is not disinterestedly objective but a means of appropriating reality to human ends. That he intended the 'dog and bone' image to be read in this way is confirmed by the 'marronnier' episode, in which Roquentin discovers, in another gastronomic image, that he cannot process material reality into thought: 'la souche noire *ne passait pas*, elle restait là, dans mes yeux, comme un morceau trop gros reste en travers d'un gosier' (p.185). One of the several meanings of 'ne pas passer' here is 'to be undigested'. The Autodidacte's entire life reflects an impossible attempt to reduce the real to the ideal: where Roquentin sees material objects, tempting dishes and flesh-and-blood people, the Autodidacte sees only the printed page, prices written on a cardboard menu and lovable abstractions.

Anny, too, expects life to conform to an idea. In her case, the idea derives from her childhood reading of Michelet's *Histoire de France*, in which certain events in history stand out because they are pictorially represented. It is, of course, the historian, aided by the artist, who has retrospectively conferred on these moments their special significance. But Anny grows up believing that such significance is intrinsic to the way in which certain privileged situations are lived through in real life itself. The 'moments parfaits' to which these situations give rise are Anny's version of what Roquentin calls adventures. There are minor differences, however. Anny's moments are more consciously modelled on the artistic enterprise. Also, much to Roquentin's misfortune, they involve other people. Whereas Roquentin compares himself to the hero of a novel, Anny is the actress-director preparing for a theatrical event. But Anny, like Roquentin, has grown disillusioned with such experiences. She had always expected life itself to provide the script for the performance. Sadly, it never did, because scripts, like values, are not already written in a 'ciel intelligible'.

These secondary characters not only contribute to the development of theme but also introduce variety of tone. The Autodidacte is a rich source of comedy. Anny, a more rounded figure, provides a human dimension which endows Roquentin with a greater measure of individuality. It is through the marginal characters, however, that the novel is most firmly rooted in the real world. For example, Sartre admirably captures the narrowness of outlook of the woman at the art gallery, when she responds to the premature death of Blévigne's son: '— Il est mort! C'est comme le fils Arondel. Il avait l'air intelligent. Ce que sa maman a dû avoir de la peine! Aussi ils en font trop dans ces grandes Ecoles. Le cerveau travaille, même pendant le sommeil. Moi, j'aime bien ces bicornes, ça fait chic' (p.134). Her unwitting demotion of the august Blévigne Junior to the same rank as the Arondels' lad also serves Sartre's satirical intentions, for it contrasts ironically with Roquentin's mock elevation of Octave Blévigne to the stature of a Virgilian hero a few lines later. As for the awe-stricken husband, his presence dramatises the theme of authority.

Form

An interesting formal feature of *La Nausée* is its dual identity as a diary and a novel. It is both a record of random occurrences characterised by the discontinuity and dispersion of day-to-day living and a novel which possesses the formal rigour of a literary masterpiece. An *Avertissement des éditeurs* draws attention to the paradox by explicitly presenting as the diary of Antoine Roquentin what the reader knows full well to be a novel by Jean-Paul Sartre. The paradox is sustained within the diary by Roquentin's insistence on the radical divorce between art and reality and by his self-exhortation to 'se méfier de la littérature' (p.85), since a literary approach would destroy the authenticity of the raw experience which he is trying to recapture verbally. The paradox is, however, easily explained. Sartre has jettisoned traditional novelistic techniques and replaced them with narrative modes that more faithfully reflect the flux of lived experience and which, accordingly, are sometimes referred to as a 'new realism'. At the same time, however, he imposes unity on the semblance of disorder by the use of techniques which belong to the symbolist tradition, techniques which seek to realise in literature the artistic purity and autonomy of a musical work.

It will be clear from the above remarks that *La Nausée* could not have been conceived along traditional lines without undermining the effect at which the diary form aims and contradicting Roquentin's distinction between life and literature. The neo-realist techniques are not at first sight visible as 'literature' because this is presented in accordance with Roquentin's conception of it as traditional and plot-centred. But how is it that the diary's 'musical' structure is able to sustain the illusion of real life? The answer is that the musical qualities of the diary's structure are as different from Roquentin's personal conception of musical form as the neo-realist techniques are from his conception of literary form. For Roquentin himself, music, like literature, has a divergent form, namely a necessary succession of notes, which opposes it to real life. Sartre's 'literary music', on the other hand, is an orchestral convergence of meaning, and can pass, on the basis of Roquentin's criteria, for the formlessness of real life. While it would be unwise to pursue too far the analogy between *La Nausée* and a musical work, it is nevertheless a useful one and will serve as a basis for the analysis of the form of *La Nausée*.

The *Feuillet sans date*, for example, is more like a musical overture than the conventional literary exposition, which sets the scene and introduces the characters. It does this, too, of course, but its principal function is to announce the work's main themes, in the manner of an operatic overture. Roquentin's disgust with the muddy underside of the pebble already points to the ambiguity objects will assume for him, to the dissolution of their identity and his fear that they might be transformed into something else. The two aspects of the pebble anticipate his predilections and revulsions. They also signal the novel's semantic scheme, which will be discussed later in this chapter. The fact that Roquentin is laughed at by children playing on the beach announces another theme: that of the outsider or non-conformist. Like a theme taken up by the different instruments or sections of an orchestra, it reappears at intervals throughout the novel, involving different characters. The Autodidacte's disgrace is the culmination of the theme. Conscious of the novel's musical structure, we are not tempted to read the incident as the unmasking of a hypocrite but as an illustration of the ferocity with which society treats the non-conformist. The incident has other meanings; it is, as it were, polyphonic. It marks, for instance, the incursion of reality into the excessively theoretical world of the Autodidacte: baited by two schoolboys, beaten up by the library attendant and verbally battered by his fellow-readers, the Autodidacte is forced to think again about the nobility of 'human nature'.

The richly varied thematic material must, of course, be made to cohere. The library scene described above illustrates one of Sartre's methods of imposing unity on the novel: he makes several themes converge in the same incident. In the same character, too: the Autodidacte is not just an outsider; his quasi-religious awe for the authority of the printed word and for the accepted canons of good taste makes him a victim of convention also. Another method is to illustrate the same theme through different characters. An important function of Anny's reunion with Roquentin is to provide a classless variation on the theme illustrated by Rogé's labelling of Achille: the bourgeois's attempt to classify, and thereby ossify, the individual. Anny's unshakable faith in Roquentin's 'essence éternelle' (p.198) is ironically contrasted by Sartre with Roquentin's acute sense of selflessness. Similarly, Anny's cultivation of perfect moments is echoed in the bourgeois's attempt to confer necessity on his existence through art: 'ils s'étaient confiés à un peintre en renom pour qu'il opérât discrètement sur leur visage ces dragages, ces forages, ces irrigations, par lesquels, tout autour de Bouville, ils avaient transformé la mer et les champs' (p.129). Anny and the bourgeois are motivated by the same fundamental desire to expel contingency from existence.

Objects constitute another ordering device in *La Nausée*. Sartre uses them to signal the reappearance of a particular theme, a technique which evokes the composer's use of the musical motif. The Autodidacte's routine snack of bread and chocolate, together with his 'linge d'une blancheur éblouissante' (p.49), identify him as a casualty of bourgeois ideology, while the shabbiness of the rest of his attire points to a lack of social integration. The three main descriptions of the bourgeoisie are linked by articles of dress and art objects. Hats feature in all three. Impétraz and his fellow-townsmen have all been idealised in bronze or paint, while those Bouvillois not yet quite dead enough to be immortalised in art perform each Sunday in the rue Tournebride 'un spectacle de qualité' (p.64). We are even taken behind the scenes of Bouville's superior brand of street-theatre by Roquentin's revelation of the sordid history of this now elegant street. When he returns the same evening, the area has the look of a deserted stage-set. His attention is caught by the creaking model of an Archbishop's mitre, which brings together in one motif the themes of social conformity (hat), art (creaking model) and religion (mitre) (p.82).

Finally, the setting itself must be seen as an integral part of the novel. Its significance is not moral but metaphysical, although critics have tended to focus exclusively on the 'Bou[e]' of Bouville with its connotation of moral condemnation. A more important function of the name is to point out the nature/ humanity opposition that runs through the novel, an opposition which is introduced at the outset in the 'pebble' episode. The muddiness of the pebble symbolises the viscosity of nature; its stoniness, the hardness of the streets and the walls of the town, a human artefact which insulates its inhabitants from the natural world. Bouville itself is divided into two distinct zones: 'Le ruban de bitume se casse net. De l'autre côté de la rue, c'est le noir et la boue... On *n'habite pas* cette région du boulevard Noir' (p.43). The opposition reaches its climax when Roquentin looks down on Bouville, before he leaves it for good, and sees that 'la grande nature vague s'est glissée dans leur ville' (p.221). The narrower settings, too, harmonise with this theme: cafés and the library are places of refuge, whereas the park and the sea provide disquieting intuitions of contingency.

Language

One of the most striking stylistic features of *La Nausée* is the frequency of images. On the whole, they portray the human as animal, or even inanimate, and the natural world as human. Their effect is to dissolve the categories in terms of which we perceive existence. Usually, an image involves a degree of mental agility, an imaginative leap from one plane or domain of reality to another. Baudelaire's images, for instance, reveal hidden similarities between things. In contrast, Roquentin's images deny obvious differences between things and are thus symptomatic of a deactivated intellect. The result is not, therefore, an enrichment of perception but a disintegration of meaning through the disappearance of an object's identity. The imagery of *La Nausée* does not reveal a secret unity, it exposes a fundamental sameness.

Inasmuch as an image depends on an explicit comparison between two terms, many of Roquentin's images are not really images at all. Even metaphor, where the comparison is only implicit, depends on the mind's retention of the invisible term. In Roquentin's case, however, what appears to be a comparison is sometimes no more than a substitution: the initial term of the comparison, even when verbally present, may become lost. Thus, the tram-seat stops being a seat before it becomes a dead donkey (pp.176-77). Another example occurs earlier in the novel, when Roquentin compares his hand to a creature which has fallen on to its back: 'Elle a l'air d'une bête à la renverse. Les doigts, ce sont les pattes' (p.141). But what he sees when he wiggles his fingers is not a hand that looks like a crab but something crablike; the hand has, in cinematic fashion, faded into a crab: 'Je m'amuse à les faire remuer, très vite, comme les pattes d'un crabe qui est tombé sur le dos' (p.141). Roquentin then stops moving his fingers and closes them over his palm: 'le crabe est mort: les pattes se recroquevillent, se ramènent sur le ventre de ma main' (p.141). The crab has taken on the familiar appearance of a clenched fist, and so becomes a hand again. In spite of Roquentin's overt comparison, what really occurs here is an oscillation from one term to the other. Ultimately, even these substitutions and oscillations will disappear, leaving only a uniform 'pâte' (p.179).

As for the second type of imagery, Roquentin's personification of nature, it obviously bears no resemblance to the pathetic fallacy of Romantic poetry. Roquentin endows nature with the least human of human characteristics: 'Toutes choses, doucement, tendrement, se laissaient aller à l'existence comme ces femmes lasses...' (p.180). Such a personification evokes, paradoxically, the inertia of inanimate objects. The dominant effect of the first type of imagery was seen to be a destructuring of existence. The second type gives prominence to existence as materiality. I mentioned earlier in the chapter that Roquentin, inasmuch as he is a body, is of a piece with the rest of existence: 'Tous les objets qui m'entouraient étaient faits de la même matière que moi, d'une espèce de souffrance moche' (p.242). The body thus becomes a privileged image of the contingency of existence as a whole. Early on in the novel, living things had been described as 'masses molles' (p.42). In the park episode, the same description is applied to inanimate, natural objects, except that, having been stripped of the structures imposed on them by consciousness, the 'bodies' are now 'unclothed': 'il restait des masses monstrueuses et molles, en désordre — nues, d'une effrayante et obscène nudité' (p.180). The only rapport between man and nature established by Roquentin's personifying imagery is, then, a distinctly 'un-Romantic', purely physical relationship.

We have seen that objects fall into two basic categories for Roquentin. His obsession with his bodily existence has the effect of polarising his view of existence into bodily and bodiless, or viscous and non-viscous. It is around this opposition, and not the philosophical *en-soi/pour-soi* opposition of *L'Etre et le néant*, that the novel revolves. Furthermore, the viscous/non-viscous opposition comes to represent an even more radical dichotomy, that between existence and art. The realm of art becomes associated with the non-viscous, while the viscous gradually permeates the whole of material reality.

Although psychology provides the main impetus for this polarisation, language plays a surprisingly active role in its consolidation, as evidenced by the following passage, which describes the Sunday outing:

> [La foule] était plus mêlée que le matin. Il semblait que tous ces hommes n'eussent plus la force de soutenir la belle hiérarchie sociale dont, avant déjeuner, ils étaient si fiers... les aristocraties, les élites, les groupements professionnels avaient fondu dans cette foule tiède. (p.78)

On the face of it, Roquentin is simply comparing two commonplace social activities: the morning walk through the exclusive rue Tournebride and the more democratic parade along the seafront. However, the choice of language turns the contrast into a series of thematic oppositions centred on the quality of viscosity.

What is, in reality, a 'mélange', becomes, with the application of a gentle heat, a 'fondu', a word which strongly suggests viscosity and which prefigures the 'affalement gélatineux' of the park episode (p.189). The heat in question is, of course, the crowd's body-heat. But it does not require the pairing of 'tiède' with 'foule' to evoke for Roquentin the temperature of the human body. At the beginning of the novel, he had felt full of 'lait tiède' (p.17). At least human existence, therefore, becomes associated at this stage with viscosity. The contrast also opposes 'fondu' and 'belle'. Although 'belle' functions, in the context, as an ironic tribute to bourgeois superiority, it nevertheless

retains its primary meaning of 'giving aesthetic pleasure', with
the result that art is, in effect, placed in the category of the non-
viscous. 'Hiérarchie', too, stands in opposition to 'fondu'. The
most obvious meaning of the passage is that the fudging of class
distinctions during the afternoon walk underlines the tenuous-
ness of social structures. The presence of 'tiède', however, adds
another dimension: the dissolution of categories in general. It
does so because 'tiédeur' evokes for Roquentin not just bodily
existence but also the nondescript drabness of real life. Neither
hot nor cold, 'tiédeur' is nauseatingly indeterminate and
suggests the underlying undifferentiatedness of the *en-soi*
generally. 'Tiède', then, in addition to being the ostensible cause
of the viscous, points to the latter's aptness as a symbol, not
only of human existence but of matter as a whole: viscosity is
indeterminate in form and texture, since it spreads in all
directions and is neither liquid nor solid.

The above passage is far from being an isolated case. Stylistically, the entire novel is structured according to a series of largely
adjectival opposites based on the viscous/non-viscous dichotomy. The name 'Bouville' itself fits neatly into this semantic
scheme. The main oppositions are soft/hard and wet/dry, and
are announced by the opening description of the pebble, which is
'sec sur tout un côté, humide et boueux sur l'autre' (p.12).

What makes softness so repulsive to Roquentin is primarily its
evocation of human flesh. It is the softness of the bodies in the
Rendez-vous des Cheminots, of 'les masses molles' (p.42), that
causes him to take flight. But 'mou' also conjures up for
Roquentin all that is repulsive in non-human as well as human
existence, which makes it doubly endearing, stylistically
speaking, to Sartre. 'Mollesse' connotes both a lack of vigour
and a lack of form — 'listlessness' is, of course, one of its
standard meanings. Human flabbiness is associated with
sluggishness and is unprepossessing to the extent that it is all
content and no form. And what makes 'mou' a fitting epithet
for existence as a whole is the fact that, for Sartre, all matter is
inert and unstructured. It is this plurality of meaning of 'mou'
which underpins Roquentin's personification of nature in the
park scene: 'Les arbres flottaient... à chaque instant je

m'attendais à voir les troncs se rider comme des verges lasses, se recroqueviller et choir sur le sol en un tas noir et mou avec des plis' (p.188).

Roquentin is also hypersensitive to wetness, whether in the form of the sea, 'un grand trou, plein d'eau noire qui remue toute seule' (p.218), or of rain, 'toute cette eau qui tombe du ciel' (p.218), or of puddles, which he is prone to stepping into (p.43). As if wet socks were not torture enough, he is also made to experience light as liquidity. His table-lamp, for instance, 'fait tout juste autour de son pied une mare pitoyable' (p.31). On walking past the lighted café windows, he takes 'trois bains de lumière jaune' (p.42). As we saw in Chapter Three, time, too, is liquefied. The depiction of insubstantial things like light and time as liquidity or viscosity provides a compelling stylistic accompaniment to Roquentin's growing awareness of material existence. The liquefaction is psychologically motivated by his preoccupation with the fluids and secretions of the body.

Predictably, objects which are hard and dry are attractive to Roquentin. On leaving the *Rendez-vous des Cheminots*, he seeks a refuge in the area beyond the avenue Galvani, where he will find only stones and earth: 'Les pierres, c'est dur et ça ne bouge pas' (p.42). Again, there are good psychological grounds for this preference, since hardness and dryness are the least human of physical qualities. The boulevard Noir, for instance, is described as 'inhumain. Comme un minéral' (p.44). Significantly, Roquentin's dream of disincarnation takes the form of a hardening and drying-out process. This is implicit from the outset in his desire to have 'ni sang ni lymphe ni chair' (p.45). It becomes more explicit at the end of the novel: 'chasser l'existence hors de moi, vider les instants de leur graisse, les tordre, les assécher, me purifier, me durcir, pour rendre enfin le son net et précis d'une note de saxophone' (pp.243-44). As elsewhere in the novel, the fluidity is uncomfortably viscous.

The coupling of 'assécher'/'durcir' with 'son net et précis' in the above quotation provides a good illustration of Sartre's identification of material existence with viscosity and of art with the non-viscous. Music, exemplified by the sound of the saxophone, is related to an absence of viscosity, in the form of a disembodied Roquentin. But for the opposition to have any force, art must be characterised not merely as an absence of viscosity but, more positively, as a presence of non-viscous qualities. This means depicting an immaterial, aesthetic object in terms of material qualities and, as far as music is concerned, establishing a close link between aural qualities and the essentially tactile and visual qualities of the non-viscous. This sensory shift is aided by certain features of material reality itself: hard objects tend to give clear sounds, hence the expression 'as clear as a bell'. But it is facilitated, too, by the flexibility of language. 'Sec' has an aural value, since we talk of a 'bruit sec' — significantly, when Roquentin compares nature to women, he describes their voices as 'mouillées' (p.180). Of course, the human voice would more naturally be described as 'nette' or 'claire' rather than 'sèche', and this makes the transition from 'assécher' and 'durcir' to 'son net et précis' a fairly smooth one.

At other times, 'sec' is applied to the notes of the song itself, when it connotes a briskness of rhythm as much as a sound quality: 'Elles courent, elles se pressent, elles me frappent au passage d'un coup sec' (p.38). Again, 'sec' aligns art with the non-viscous, especially since the rhythm is contrasted with the ponderous gesture of the card-player: 'ce geste... qui ramasse les cartes en trébuchant: il est tout flasque' (p.38), a description which is evocative of the softness of the body and the sluggish-ness of things viscous. The quotation in question makes one further contribution to the existence/art opposition. Not only would a non-viscous Roquentin give rise to a musical sound that is 'net et précis', but these adjectives themselves evoke visual and conceptual clarity, for we talk of 'idées nettes' and 'contours nets'. Existence, on the other hand, is 'floue' (p.33) and 'vague' (p.32).

'Dur', which is more restricted in its range of meanings than 'sec', can nevertheless apply to sounds, and does so when Roquentin hears an electric bell which is 'plus dure, moins humaine que les autres bruits' (p.44). The phrase marks a pre-liminary stage in the polarisation of existence and art by establishing hardness as a non-human quality. But usually, when Roquentin applies 'dur' to music, it is not to describe a sound quality at all but formal rigour. In other words, 'dur' is given a metaphorical dimension, a dimension which will allow Roquentin to characterise his projected novel as 'belle et dure comme de l'acier' (p.247). Elsewhere, the temporal necessity (*durée*) of music and literature is portrayed more conventionally, but less evocatively, as 'un ordre inflexible' (p.38) and 'un enchaînement rigoureux' (p.41).

In the section of *L'Etre et le néant* which deals with existential psychoanalysis, Sartre interprets aversion to viscosity as a consciousness's fear of being sucked into the *en-soi*: 'L'horreur du visqueux c'est l'horreur que le temps [consciousness as temporality] ne devienne visqueux, que la facticité [material existence as 'fact-ness' or 'made-ness'] ne progresse continûment et insensiblement et n'aspire le Pour-soi qui ''l'existe''' (*6*, p.702). But *La Nausée* is a novel and not a psychological case-study, and so the significance of viscosity is not made to depend on psychoanalysis. Rather, viscosity symbolises bodily existence and the structureless *en-soi*. There is, understandably, an overlap between the two works. There are times when Roquentin has to shake himself free or tear himself away from his fascination with material reality. Conversely, *L'Etre et le néant* itself stresses the indeterminacy of viscosity, which has 'un caractère louche de ''substance entre deux états''' (*6*, p.699).

Owing to its double symbolic value, therefore, viscosity is not only central to the novel's psychological dimension but integrates it with the philosophical dimension. It allows a graphic description of, one might even say 'fleshes out', the philosophical distinction between art and existence, between necessity and contingency, by enabling material existence and the immaterial work of art to be accommodated within the same lexical scheme. It is also viscosity that establishes a link between nausea and contingency. In *L'Etre et le néant*, the undifferentiated nature of the *en-soi* is arrived at philosophically. In *La Nausée*, the psychological obsession leads directly to the revelation of brute, undifferentiated being. The twofold significance of viscosity allows the novel's psychological climax to converge with the moment of philosophical insight. Structurally speaking, viscosity does a thoroughly good sticking job.

Conclusion: La Nausée *and the Literary Tradition*

The contrast between existence and art is given a literary formulation both through Roquentin's reflections on his 'adventures' and through a number of allusions which situate *La Nausée* in relation to the French literary tradition. These allusions provide a counterpoint to the diary, through which the authorial voice, as distinct from Roquentin's, develops the life/literature theme. The allusive dimension would have been announced by the very title of the novel, had Gallimard taken up either of the two titles proposed by Sartre himself, since 'Melancholia' refers explicitly to an engraving by Dürer and 'Les Aventures extraordinaires d'Antoine Roquentin' evokes the classic adventure-story. Owing to the adoption of 'La Nausée' as the novel's title, however, the *Avertissement des éditeurs* alone has to fulfil the function of alerting the reader to this dual perspective of diary and novel. The *avertissement* is able to function in this way because it at once conceals literariness (*37*, pp.228-30; *3*, p.1719) and displays it (*36*, p.3; *40*, pp.42-44). It does the former by conferring on the diary the open-endedness of real life, in that it raises questions about Roquentin's ultimate fate which are destined to remain unanswered. It displays literariness to the extent that it is recognisable as a well-worn fictional device. Thus, two distinct narrative levels are maintained simultaneously: a realistic, diary level — the novel as narrated by Roquentin — and a self-conscious, fictional level — the novel written by Sartre. In this way, *La Nausée* draws attention to itself as an 'anti-' or 'new' novel. It explicitly compares itself with two works: an eighteenth-century novel by Lesage, *Histoire de Gil Blas de Santillane*, and a novel of the nineteenth century, Balzac's *Eugénie Grandet*.

The novel of the eighteenth century is an appropriate point of departure for Sartre's critique of traditional literature since it gives a high priority to story-telling. It is a reference to Lesage's novel (p.58) that introduces Roquentin's crucial distinction between 'vivre' and 'raconter' (p.62), a fact which attests to the importance of the allusive infrastructure of *La Nausée*. Roquentin discovers at this point that there are no 'histoires vraies' (p.63), the reason being that retrospective narration profoundly alters an experience by imposing upon it a significance and coherence which did not exist at the time of its occurrence. Roquentin illustrates the difference between 'living' and 'telling' by remarking of his affair with Erna in Hamburg: 'J'étais dedans, je n'y pensais pas' (p.62). The difference corresponds approximately to the philosophical distinction between primary and secondary or reflective consciousness, outlined in Chapter Three. Owing to the presence of *Gil Blas*, the difference becomes one of narrative technique.

In an *avertissement* ('Gil Blas au lecteur'), itself anecdotal in character, Gil Blas refers to his 'aventures' and presents the novel as 'l'histoire de [sa] vie'. In other words, he is a 'conteur d'histoires' (p.62) who, from the vantage-point of old age, is able to survey his life as a whole and so narrate it in the light of its (near-) end. The mode of narration is the traditional first-person past historic. It stands in obvious contrast to the first-person present of Roquentin's *journal intime*. The narrating of experiences in the form of a diary is close to the moment of their occurrence. In Roquentin's case, there is sometimes simultaneity even, as when he abandons the diary convention altogether in favour of the 'stream of consciousness' technique.

In addition to creating a difference of narrative perspective, the plot-centredness of the eighteenth-century novel also opposes it structurally to Sartre's novel. In contrast to the closed form of Lesage's novel, *La Nausée* is open-ended. What little plot there is creates an impression of disjointedness and has neither a clear-cut beginning nor a conclusive ending. The diary is preceded by an isolated, undated page, which functions, structurally, as a false start. The plot does not so much build up as break down. Roquentin's eagerly awaited reunion with Anny is a non-event. The downfall of the Autodidacte, the only real event in the entire novel, is not the culmination of a carefully prepared progression but a thunderbolt out of a blue sky, made all the more unexpected by Roquentin's confident predictions of the Autodidacte's future: 'Demain soir, après-demain soir, tous les soirs qui suivraient, il reviendrait lire à cette table en mangeant son pain et son chocolat' (p.226). The novel ends with Roquentin's future still in the balance, as he contemplates, with some hesitation, the possibility of writing a novel. The ending calls to mind the last paragraph of *Les Caves du Vatican*, where Gide, equally reluctant to seal Lafcadio's fate, explicitly declares: 'Ici commence un nouveau livre'. But the last paragraph of Gide's novel, by its very announcement of a new departure for Lafcadio, constitutes an ending of a kind. *La Nausée* is more radical. Even the slender possibility of a fresh start for Roquentin is too decisive a note on which to conclude. And so, Sartre's novel ends with a deliberate anti-climax: the nauseating prospect of yet another rainy day in Bouville. Such an ending reflects the shapelessness of real life and sums up the entire 'action': 'Quand on vit, il n'arrive rien... Il n'y a jamais de commencements. Les jours s'ajoutent aux jours sans rime ni raison, c'est une addition interminable et monotone... Il n'y a pas de fin non plus...' (p.62).

Eugénie Grandet is Roquentin's constant companion. While reading the novel in the Brasserie Vézelize, he is distracted by a conversation at the next table which just happens to provide a basis for comparison with the page he has turned to (p.74). In the manuscript version of *La Nausée*, the extract from *Eugénie Grandet* and the 'real-life' *brasserie* conversation are explicitly compared by Roquentin: 'Le dialogue des romans, où chacun répond exactement à son interlocuteur, comme c'est loin du vrai langage des gens' (*3*, p.1763). The omission of this sentence from the published version is revealing. Its retention would have strait-jacketed the reader's response. For Roquentin, the significance of the juxtaposition is confined to the immediately obvious: the discrepancy between the sporadic, incoherent conversations of real life and the ordered precision of dialogue in novels. For him, *Eugénie Grandet* is purely and simply a novel that illustrates the difference between life and art. For the reader, however, attuned to Sartre's ploy of setting *La Nausée* against traditional literature, *Eugénie Grandet* is a nineteenth-century realist novel that demonstrates the failure of realism to represent reality with accuracy. Moreover, it is not only the dialogue which is stylised. Whereas Eugénie channels her dawning love for her cousin into the commendable desire to serve him a strong cup of coffee at lunchtime, her 'real-life' counterpart combines matters of the heart and of the table with considerably less delicacy: 'Charles, tais-toi, tu m'excites, mon chéri, murmure-t-elle en souriant, la bouche pleine' (p.76). In comparison with the café conversation, the Balzac extract reads like a bowdlerisation of reality (*30*, pp.14-16).

In the nineteenth-century novel, the centre of interest shifts from plot to character. Roquentin reaches the same conclusion about the latter as about the former: traditional literary categories do not accurately reflect lived experience. The Autodidacte is instrumental in this discovery. The effect of Roquentin's refusal to use his name is to establish him as a literary type, evocative not only of the monolithic characters of Balzac's novels but also of the classical tradition. Roquentin realises the inadequacy of such literary labelling, which reduces a complex human being to a single character-trait, during his lunch with the Autodidacte. When the latter reminisces about his war-time experiences, Roquentin is taken aback: 'Je ne puis me l'imaginer autrement qu'autodidacte' (p.150). After the Autodidacte's public disgrace, the label will become inapplicable to his future also, since thereafter he will be debarred from using the public library.

The relation of *La Nausée* to twentieth-century fiction is both more complex and more elusive. The self-conscious rejection of traditional fiction gives *La Nausée* a Gidean flavour, as does the caricatural presentation of the Autodidacte. The preoccupation with human subjectivity at the expense of external events aligns it with Proust's *A la recherche du temps perdu*: both novels are shaped by a gradual expansion of the narrator's consciousness. The two novels also share thematic preoccupations, such as the possibility of redemption through art. Although Sartre himself once indicated that both Rilke and Valéry had influenced *La Nausée*, it is undoubtedly Proust's novel to which it owes most. A discussion of the relationship between the two works is beyond the scope of the present study, but it is as well to point out, perhaps, that *La Nausée* is not, as critics have sometimes argued, a straightforward parody of *A la recherche du temps perdu* (*41*, pp.348-51).

As for Sartre's successors, the 'new novelists', they clearly owe a debt to *La Nausée*. Its literary self-consciousness, its calling into question of plot and character, its stress on the problematic relation of language to reality make it a precursor of the *nouveau roman* (*19*, pp.1-6). As Georges Raillard notes in the *Avant-propos* to his study of *La Nausée*, 'par ce livre s'est... poursuivi l'ébranlement d'une certaine conception du roman français. Ebranlement qui, au reste, a plus bénéficié aux romanciers français qui auront lu *La Nausée* qu'à Sartre lui-même si l'on en juge par *Les Chemins de la liberté*' (*40*). This suggests that Sartre, having reverted, after *La Nausée*, to a more traditional approach to fiction, failed to fulfil his earlier promise as a novelist, a suggestion which Sartre's own preference for *La Nausée* appears to endorse.

From Sartre's own point of view, however, there was no agonising choice to be made between pure and committed literature. The largely formal preoccupations of the new novelists led to a kind of literature which was too restricted in scope for a writer of Sartre's tastes. Even *La Nausée*, in spite of its literary self-consciousness, had philosophical and moral dimensions which were served rather than contested by its literary dimension. As for Sartre's later characters, they inhabit a wholly human world of interpersonal relations with its concomitant moral dilemmas. It was less a case of the socialist bullying the writer into abandoning the path of pure literature than of the writer/philosopher choosing a subject-matter to which the preoccupations of the *nouveau romancier* were hardly relevant. Sartre's 'literary regression' was, in his own eyes, a philosophical progression. Not the least of Sartre's personal qualities were a total absence of pretentiousness and a strong commitment to truth and to social justice. It was typical of Sartre the man to have placed philosophical and moral convictions above the standing of Sartre the innovative artist.

Select Bibliography

The most recent bibliography of critical material on Sartre's works is: François H. Lapointe, *Jean-Paul Sartre and his Critics: an international bibliography (1938-1980)*, second edition (Ohio, Bowling Green State University, 1981).

EDITIONS OF LA NAUSEE

1. *La Nausée*, Collection Folio (Paris, Gallimard, 1970).
2. *La Nausée*, Collection Blanche (Paris, Gallimard, 1938).
3. *Œuvres romanesques*, edited by Michel Contat and Michael Rybalka, Bibliothèque de la Pléiade (Paris, Gallimard, 1981). Indispensable for detailed study of *La Nausée*.

OTHER WORKS BY SARTRE CITED IN THE TEXT

4. *La Transcendance de l'Ego, esquisse d'une description phénoménologique*, ed. Sylvie Le Bon (Paris, Vrin, 1965). First published in 1937.
5. *L'Imaginaire, psychologie phénoménologique de l'imagination* (Paris, Gallimard, 1940).
6. *L'Etre et le néant, essai d'ontologie phénoménologique* (Paris, Gallimard, 1943).
7. *Being and Nothingness: an essay on phenomenological ontology*, translated by Hazel E. Barnes (New York, Philosophical Library, 1956). Contains a useful introduction.
8. *L'Existentialisme est un humanisme* (Paris, Nagel, 1946).
9. 'Une Idée fondamentale de la phénoménologie de Husserl: l'intentionnalité', in *Situations I* (Paris, Gallimard, 1947), pp.31-35. The essay was written in 1939.
10. 'Qu'est-ce que la littérature?', in *Situations II* (Paris, Gallimard, 1948), pp.55-330.
11. 'Matérialisme et révolution', in *Situations III* (Paris, Gallimard, 1949), pp.135-225.
12. *Les Mots* (Paris, Gallimard, 1964).

INTERVIEWS GIVEN BY SARTRE

13. Jacqueline Piatier, 'Jean-Paul Sartre s'explique sur *Les Mots*', *Le Monde*, 18 avril 1964, p.13.
14. *Sartre*, un film réalisé par Alexandre Astruc et Michel Contat (Paris, Gallimard, 1977). Most of the film was shot in 1972.

15. 'Autoportrait à soixante-dix ans', in *Situations X* (Paris, Gallimard, 1976), pp.133-226. The interviewer was Michel Contat.

BIOGRAPHICAL AND BACKGROUND MATERIAL

16. Beauvoir, Simone de, *Mémoires d'une jeune fille rangée* (Paris, Gallimard, 1958).
17. ——, *La Force de l'âge* (Paris, Gallimard, 1960).
18. Copleston, F.C., 'The existentialism of Sartre', in *A History of Philosophy*, IX, *Maine de Biran to Sartre* (London, Search Press, 1975), pp.368-89.
19. Jefferson, Ann, *The Nouveau Roman and the Poetics of Fiction* (Cambridge University Press, 1980).
20. Vernon, M.D., *The Psychology of Perception* (London, Penguin, 1962).

GENERAL STUDIES OF SARTRE

21. Champigny, Robert, *Stages on Sartre's Way, 1938-1952* (New York, Kraus Reprint Corporation, 1974). Originally published in 1959 by Indiana University Press.
22. Goldthorpe, Rhiannon, *Sartre: literature and theory*, Cambridge Studies in French (Cambridge University Press, 1984). Not for the novice.
23. Jameson, Fredric, *Sartre:the origins of a style* (New Haven, Yale University Press, 1961).
24. Jeanson, Francis, *Sartre par lui-même*, Collection Ecrivains de toujours, 29 (Paris, Seuil, 1955).
25. Manser, Anthony, *Sartre: a philosophic study* (London, Athlone Press, 1966).
26. Murdoch, Iris, *Sartre: romantic rationalist*, Studies in Modern European Literature and Thought (London, Bowes and Bowes, 1953).
27. Prince, J.G., *Métaphysique et technique dans l'œuvre romanesque de Sartre* (Geneva, Droz, 1968).

CRITICAL STUDIES OF LA NAUSEE

28. Ansel, Yves, *'La Nausée' de Jean-Paul Sartre*, Collection Lectoguide second cycle (Paris, Bordas, 1982). Sixth-form level.
29. Bauer, George, *'La Nausée*: melancholy of the artist', in *Sartre and the Artist* (Chicago University Press, 1969), pp.13-44.
30. Edwards, Michael, *'La Nausée* — a symbolist novel', *Adam*, 35 (1970), 9-21.
31. Fitch, Brian T., 'Le mirage du moi idéal: *La Nausée* de Jean-Paul Sartre', in *Le Sentiment d'étrangeté chez Malraux, Sartre, Camus, Simone de Beauvoir* (Paris, Minard, 1964), pp.95-139.
32. Fletcher, D.J., 'The use of colour in *La Nausée*', *Modern Language Review*, 63 (1968), 370-80.

33. Frohock, W.M., 'Sartre in *La Nausée*', in *Style and Temper: studies in French fiction, 1925-1960* (Oxford, Blackwell, 1967), pp.94-103.

34. Gore, Keith, *Sartre: 'La Nausée' and 'Les Mouches'*, Studies in French Literature, 17, second edition (London, Arnold, 1974).

35. Idt, Geneviève, *'La Nausée' de Sartre*, Collection Profil d'une œuvre, 18 (Paris, Hatier, 1971).

36. ——, '*Les Mots*, sans les choses, sans les mots, *La Nausée*', *Degrés*, I (1973), 1-17.

37. Keefe, Terry, 'The ending of Sartre's *La Nausée*', *Forum for Modern Language Studies*, XII (1976), 217-35.

38. Magny, Claude-Edmonde, 'Sartre ou la duplicité de l'être: ascèse et mythomanie', in *Les Sandales d'Empédocle: essai sur les limites de la littérature* (Neuchâtel, La Baconnière, 1945), pp.105-72.

39. Poulet, Georges, '*La Nausée* de Sartre', in *Etudes sur le temps humain*, 3: *Le Point de départ* (Paris, Editions du Rocher, 1977), pp.216-36.

40. Raillard, Georges, *'La Nausée' de Jean-Paul Sartre*, Collection Poche Critique, 4 (Paris, Hachette, 1972). Not easy, but worth the effort.

41. Reed, Paul and McLure, Roger, '*La Nausée* and the problem of literary representation', *Modern Language Review*, 82 (1987), 343-55.

42. Spanos, William V., 'The postmodernity of Sartre's *La Nausée*', *Criticism*, XX (1978), 223-80.

CRITICAL GUIDES TO FRENCH TEXTS

edited by
Roger Little, Wolfgang van Emden, David Williams

1. **David Bellos.** Balzac: La Cousine Bette
2. **Rosemarie Jones.** Camus: L'Etranger *and* La Chute
3. **W.D. Redfern.** Queneau: Zazie dans le métro
4. **R.C. Knight.** Corneille: Horace
5. **Christopher Todd.** Voltaire: Dictionnaire philosophique
6. **J.P. Little.** Beckett: En attendant Godot *and* Fin de partie
7. **Donald Adamson.** Balzac: Illusions perdues
8. **David Coward.** Duras: Moderato cantabile
9. **Michael Tilby.** Gide: Les Faux-Monnayeurs
10. **Vivienne Mylne.** Diderot: La Religieuse
11. **Elizabeth Fallaize.** Malraux: La Voie royale
12. **H.T. Barnwell.** Molière: Le Malade imaginaire
13. **Graham E. Rodmell.** Marivaux: Le Jeu de l'amour et du hasard *and* Les Fausses Confidences
14. **Keith Wren.** Hugo: Hernani *and* Ruy Blas
15. **Peter S. Noble.** Beroul's Tristan *and the* Folie de Berne
16. **Paula Clifford.** Marie de France: Lais
17. **David Coward.** Marivaux: La Vie de Marianne *and* Le Paysan parvenu
18. **J.H. Broome.** Molière: L'Ecole des femmes *and* Le Misanthrope
19..**B.G. Garnham.** Robbe-Grillet: Les Gommes *and* Le Voyeur
20. **J.P. Short.** Racine: Phèdre
21. **Robert Niklaus.** Beaumarchais: Le Mariage de Figaro
22. **Anthony Cheal Pugh.** Simon: Histoire
23. **Lucie Polak.** Chrétien de Troyes: Cligés
24. **John Cruickshank.** Pascal: Pensées
25. **Ceri Crossley.** Musset: Lorenzaccio
26. **J.W. Scott.** Madame de Lafayette: La Princesse de Clèves
27. **John Holyoake.** Montaigne: Essais
28. **Peter Jimack.** Rousseau: Emile
29. **Roger Little.** Rimbaud: Illuminations
30. **Barbara Wright and David Scott.** Baudelaire: La Fanfarlo *and* Le Spleen de Paris

31. **Haydn Mason.** Cyrano de Bergerac: L'Autre Monde
32. **Glyn S. Burgess.** Chrétien de Troyes: Erec et Enide
33. **S. Beynon John.** Anouilh: L'Alouette *and* Pauvre Bitos
34. **Robin Buss.** Vigny: Chatterton
35. **David Williams.** Rousseau: Les Rêveries du promeneur
     solitaire
36. **Ronnie Butler.** Zola: La Terre
37. **John Fox.** Villon: Poems
38. **C.E.J. Dolamore.** Ionesco: Rhinocéros
39. **Robert Lethbridge.** Maupassant: Pierre et Jean
40. **David Curtis.** Descartes: Discours de la Méthode
41. **Peter Cogman.** Hugo: Les Contemplations
42. **Rosemary Lloyd.** Mallarmé: Poésies
43. **M. Adereth.** Aragon: The Resistance Poems
44. **Keith Wren.** Vigny: Les Destinées
45. **Kathleen M. Hall and Margaret B. Wells.** Du Bellay: Poems
46. **Geoffrey Bremner.** Diderot: Jacques le fataliste
47. **Peter Dunwoodie.** Camus: L'Envers et l'Endroit *and* L'Exil
     et le Royaume
48. **Michael Sheringham.** Beckett: Molloy
49. **J.F. Falvey.** Diderot: Le Neveu de Rameau